Living Spaces for Children

By the Editors of Time-Life Books

Alexandria, Virginia

TIME® LIFE BOOKS

Library of Congress Cataloging in Publication Data
Living spaces for children.
 (Successful parenting)
 Bibliography: p.
 Includes index.
 1. Children's rooms. 2. Interior decoration.
I. Time-Life Books.   II. Series.
NK2117.C4L58 1988   747.7'7   88-2287
ISBN 0-8094-5954-X
ISBN 0-8094-5955-8 (lib. bdg.)

Successful Parenting

SERIES DIRECTOR: Dale M. Brown
Series Administrator: Jane Edwin
Editorial Staff for *Living Spaces:*
Designer: Elissa E. Baldwin
Picture Editor: Jane Jordan
Text Editors: Margery A. duMond, John Newton,
Moira J. Saucer
Researchers: Karen Monks (principal), Sydney
Johnson, Mary McCarthy
Assistant Designer: Susan M. Gibas
Copy Coordinators: Marfé Ferguson Delano,
Charles J. Hagner
Picture Coordinator: Betty Weatherley
Editorial Assistant: Jayne A. L. Dover

Special Contributors: Amy Aldrich, Wendy Mur-
phy, Charles C. Smith (text); Anne Muñoz-Furlong
(research); Louise Hedberg (index); Jayne E. Roh-
rich (copyediting)

Editorial Operations
Copy Chief: Diane Ullius
Production: Celia Beattie
Library: Louise D. Forstall

Correspondents: Elisabeth Kraemer-Singh (Bonn);
Maria Vincenza Aloisi (Paris); Ann Natanson
(Rome)

Other Publications:

THE TIME-LIFE GARDENER'S GUIDE
MYSTERIES OF THE UNKNOWN
TIME FRAME
FIX IT YOURSELF
FITNESS, HEALTH & NUTRITION
HEALTHY HOME COOKING
UNDERSTANDING COMPUTERS
LIBRARY OF NATIONS
THE ENCHANTED WORLD
THE KODAK LIBRARY OF CREATIVE
 PHOTOGRAPHY
GREAT MEALS IN MINUTES
THE CIVIL WAR
PLANET EARTH
COLLECTOR'S LIBRARY OF THE CIVIL WAR
THE EPIC OF FLIGHT
THE GOOD COOK
WORLD WAR II
HOME REPAIR AND IMPROVEMENT
THE OLD WEST

*For information on and a full description of any
of the Time-Life Books series listed above, please
call 1-800-621-7026 or write:*
Reader Information
Time-Life Customer Service
P.O. Box C-32068
Richmond, Virginia 23261-2068

This volume is one of a series about raising
children.

The Consultants

General Consultants

Dr. Robert H. Bradley, a consultant for the first four sections of this book, is Director of the Center for Research on Teaching and Learning and Adjunct Professor of Pediatrics at the University of Arkansas at Little Rock. He helped develop the Home Observation for Measurement of the Environment (HOME) Inventory, a guide used extensively by pediatric, public health, and early-education professionals to determine the quality of both the physical and the emotional home environments of children and how they affect children's well-being. Dr. Bradley has written many articles on this subject and has been a contributor to numerous books, including *Play Interactions* and *Early Child Development and Care.* Among his other professional affiliations, he is a member of the Society for Research in Child Development and the American Psychological Association.

Martin E. Rich advised on ways in which parents can create the most beneficial physical surroundings for their children (sections one through four). An architect and head of his own firm in New York City, Mr. Rich has extensive experience in designing living environments for youngsters, with specific emphasis on converting small, marginal spaces into bedroom and play areas that are functional, imaginative, and stimulating. His work has been featured in numerous periodicals, including *AIA Journal, The New York Times Magazine,* and *Metropolitan Home.* Mr. Rich has taught architecture at several schools, including the New York Institute of Technology; he is also a member of the American Institute of Architects.

Special Consultants

Mary Ellen R. Fise provided guidance for sections two and five concerning child safety in the home. A lawyer and Product Safety Director for the Consumer Federation of America, the nation's largest consumer-advocacy organization, she represents CFA on safety- and health-related issues before governmental regulatory agencies. Ms. Fise is coauthor of the book *The Childwise Catalog: Buying the Safest and Best Products for Your Children* and a member of the adjunct faculty at Boston University, where she teaches a course on consumer protection law.

Dr. Theodore D. Wachs, who gave his expert view on the importance of an orderly environment in a young child's life *(page 74),* is a professor in the Department of Psychological Sciences at Purdue University. He has done extensive research on the relationship between the physical environment of infants and toddlers and their cognitive development, and the results of his work have been published in many scholarly journals. Dr. Wachs is also coauthor of the book *Early Experience and Human Development,* as well as a fellow of the American Psychological Association and a member of the Society for Research in Child Development.

Contents

4 Play Spaces to Suit Your Child   98

5 Safety First   118

Thinking Small

Think small, not big. That is the common-sense advice that experts give when it comes to creating living spaces for children. Yet all too often it is advice that goes ignored, even among some of the best-intentioned of parents, who forget that their child has some very special needs of her own in terms of the home environment. The best way to avoid such a mistake in planning your own youngster's living spaces—her bedroom, her play areas, her bathroom, or any other part of the house she frequents—is to see the world from her perspective. Get down on your hands and knees in each room and look around. Try to perceive the room as she does. You may discover that you have booby-trapped the environment unwittingly, leaving all sorts of dangers and temptations in her way. Or you may find that you have arranged things in a manner that can only frustrate her, denying her a feeling of mastery and control. The clothes rack may be beyond her grasp, the light switches too high, the floor a maze of furniture without enough open space for freewheeling play.

Once you have examined your home from your child's viewpoint, you will be in a better position to modify it appropriately and to make intelligent choices when designing and furnishing those special areas that will belong to her alone. Conceived to make your decorating easier, this chapter contains practical advice on room layouts, scaling furnishings down to size, color, floor surfaces, and what works best and why. As the picture opposite demonstrates, with a little ingenuity and a few decorative flourishes, even a tiny attic corner can become a child's cozy getaway.

The Nurturing Space of Your Home

In a sense, a young child's immediate environment is her whole world. Her most important milestones—from her first bath to her first telephone call—take place in the nurturing space of your home. Every room is a personal laboratory where your child can test new ideas about the world, a nesting ground where she can experience the joy and encouragement of positive social encounters with the rest of the family. Since an ideal learning environment for a child allows her constantly to explore her surroundings, put her ideas to work, and develop her sense of self, you will probably find yourself wanting to tailor as many aspects of your apartment or house to your growing youngster's needs as possible.

In planning your child's living space, bear in mind that it should reflect a quality the experts call responsiveness. A responsive environment is one in which your youngster's needs are anticipated, her efforts reinforced, and her requests for assistance consistently met. It is also one where things are visible and accessible to her. It contains a variety of manipulable objects in good working order, to encourage her to explore without frustration. And it is a relatively quiet environment, free from unwanted distractions. In other words, it is a home in which a youngster can thrive, gaining a sense of self and of proprietorship.

You need not bend over backward to modify your home from top to bottom for your child's sake, but since she is so much a part of your daily life, you may wish to make some basic accommodations that will save you both frustrations. You may choose, for example, to live with durable furniture and simple accessories while she is young and spirited and acquire finer pieces later. To encourage exploration without frustration or danger, you should keep breakables out of her reach and remove any hazards. And to help her feel that she can make her own contribution to the warm atmosphere of the family home, you will do well to hang samples of her artwork on the walls or a kitchen bulletin board.

A child's haven
While a child should feel that he is welcome anywhere in the home, even a toddler must have a spot set aside as his very own. It should be a place that he can enjoy, and it should be exciting enough to

stimulate different aspects of his development. It should also be a safe haven where he can feel free to do much as he pleases. Children need time to themselves for daydreaming and other solitary play activities—looking at picture books, listening to music, painting, drawing, or simply gazing out the window from a comfortable chair.

Once your youngster is old enough to play without your constant supervision, set up his bedroom or play area as a cozy refuge that expresses his tastes and preferences. A child flourishes where toys, books, and decoration capture his eye and engage his imagination. Ideally, your child's living space should be flexible, able to grow with him as he advances from infancy to adolescence.

Children often have strong territorial urges; they may make a point of marking off boundaries or claiming certain areas for themselves—the eaves, the storage area under the front stairs, a corner of the basement. Your child will early on demonstrate an attachment to his room. Do not be surprised if he insists on changing or rearranging it. Make sure, therefore, that some of the furniture is light enough for him to move. Putting your child's name on his bedroom door is one way you can confirm that this is indeed his space. While it is important for you to understand your child's natural attachment to his special place, be sure to let him know that it is he who makes it special. Such an attitude helps a child feel more secure should the time come to move to a new bedroom or perhaps a new house. As you work with your youngster to develop his domain, you will be doing something more—helping him acquire the skills and attitudes that he must have in order to feel at home when he is grown-up. ⁘

This little girl's parents have given her just what she needs—a playhouse of her own under the basement stairs. At some point, your child will probably discover an unused space and convert it into a hiding place or a secret clubhouse available only to other children.

9

The Whys and Wherefores of Room Planning

Creating a suitable bedroom or playroom for your child is a challenging but pleasant job that will yield rewards for years to come. But before you get started on any building, remodeling, or even redecorating project, take some time to think carefully about the project. Be sure you know exactly how much you can afford and exactly what you hope to accomplish.

Many factors come into play when you consider changes in any household space. If your child is very young, safety concerns will be of paramount importance in designing the room. You will want to arrange things so that your infant or toddler cannot climb out a window, stick a finger in an electrical outlet, or run into furniture with sharp edges or corners. Once these concerns are taken care of, you can devote yourself to the exciting task of decorating your youngster's room. Even if you have little money, you can use imagination and ingenuity to create a space your child will love. Some inexpensive curtains, accessories, and secondhand furniture painted bright colors are often enough to do the trick.

These children are busily being themselves in a remodeled attic that doubles as bedroom and play area. Daybeds against the walls leave space in the center of the room for quiet play or vigorous exercise on a portable seesaw. A toy kitchen set transforms an alcove into a space for imaginative play.

Inevitably, any decorating project will have to take into account your future family plans. Perhaps you intend to have more children, in which case you should choose furniture and play equipment that will survive the rough treatment it will get. Will one child be using the room for many years? If so, you should plan for changes of décor as she grows. Although juvenile furniture may appeal to both you and your youngster, consider that in just a few years the very same child will be eager to graduate to furnishings that suit her more grown-up social needs. Remember, also, that it will be less time than you think before such items as telephones, stereo systems, and personal computers find their way into your child's life—and her room. Bear in mind, too, the possibility that you will be moving to a new home within a few years, in which case fur-

nishings that can be transported easily and adapted conveniently to a new space may be in order. The length of time you intend to stay in your present home can affect your design decisions in other ways. For example, you may decide against installing permanent features such as built-in cabinets. And if you rent your home, there may be restrictions in your lease that limit your building, painting, and wallpapering options.

As a further practicality, take stock of your own feelings about a child's room, especially in regard to gender. Do you have strong feelings about which color schemes or accessories are appropriate for boys and girls? The choices you make are bound to have some impact on your child's activities, feelings, and development. Perhaps you would like to give your little girl a frilly room, when in fact she loves romping about in her old clothes with friends and pets. Ideally, you should seek a balance between your youngster's interests and your ideas about what is gender appropriate.

With such considerations in mind, you can begin the fun and creative part of your job: deciding the best use for your child's space. Keep in mind the room's purpose and what activities will take place there. Will the bedroom be for sleeping and a separate playroom for playing, or will the bedroom serve for both activities? Your child can help you; she may

be able to describe in words her ideal room, although she may still be too young to explain very well her likes and dislikes. Consider spending some time observing her and taking some mental notes as she plays; this may clue you in to the kind of room she might enjoy. A child shifts gears often; in several hours, you will probably see her move through a number of activities. Watching her, you will get an idea of the kind of play she prefers, her general interests, and her involvement; as well, take note of the colors she gravitates toward in crayons and paints.

For a toddler who spends much of her time in active physical play or on pretend activities, plenty of open floor space and accessible toys are in order. The slightly older child, who enjoys being alone in her room looking at books, quietly painting, or playing with modeling clay, will need a comfortable chair, good lighting, and a work area with easy-to-clean surfaces. If your child is an active one and has reached the age where her friends are around to join her in continuous and rambunctious motion—running, climbing, and jumping wherever space permits—give her as much room as possible, plenty of soft edges, few breakables, and movable furniture. You may notice that your child likes to dress up in your old clothes, to dance, or to play with puppets; perhaps she needs a space to show family and friends her fantasies.

With insights like these to guide you, your job will be easier. Try to engage your child in the project. Ask her where she would like her storage chest, her lamp, her worktable. Sound her out about decorations that would appeal to her interests; show her pictures in catalogs or make it a treat for her to go with you to yard sales or stores to turn up interesting items.

You will probably find it necessary to consider the needs of other family members in your planning. If your child must share her living and play spaces with a sibling, room dividers or appropriately arranged storage pieces can help establish privacy. If you have live-in grandparents or older or younger children with rooms of their own, you will want to take into account how noisy activities will impinge on them. Choose the location of the room carefully, and consider using wall coverings and carpets, if necessary, to cut down on the decibel level. Similar considerations will arise if you work at home and need a place to meet with clients well away from the sounds of an active, happy child at play.

Where consideration of others is involved, neatness may count as much as noise control. Consider your own need to conserve your energy for all your many responsibilities, and

Noting their child's preference for primary colors, a couple has decorated his room with vivid red, yellow, and blue, set off by white walls and green carpeting.

decide who will be responsible for keeping the room tidy. If you expect your child to pick up after play, then she should be able to reach the shelves and other areas where her toys and belongings are kept.

In some families, the special physical requirements of a child must be taken into account. For children with health problems or physical disabilities, the room design should reflect their needs in specific ways. The child who suffers from severe allergies, for instance, will require a dust-free room. This means not only keeping it scrupulously clean, but also eliminating down-filled pillows and comforters, stuffed animals, thick pile carpets, and heavy bedspreads—anything that might collect and harbor dust.

If a child has to negotiate the home in a wheelchair, it will be necessary to provide wide enough doorways and ample spaces between the furniture. Since small area rugs impede movement, they should be avoided, and all mirrors and pictures should be hung at the child's eye level. Similarly, lighting, shelves, and drawers should be reachable from a sitting position. Fortunately, special furniture can be purchased for the use of the handicapped child.

A youngster with a visual impairment may need powerful lighting in some areas of the room. For a completely blind child, textures will be an important part of room décor; different paints and wallpapers can give each section of wall its own distinctive feel.

Other considerations arise if your child divides her time between the homes of two parents. She will need her own personal space in both households and will very likely keep clothing, a toothbrush, and other basic items at each place. The parent who lives apart from the family should do the utmost to make the child feel at home by giving her a storage space to call her own—a trunk, an alcove, or part of a closet will suffice—and by providing age-appropriate toys, books, and art supplies. One parent may be stricter than the other about neatness, but such differences do not have to be a problem. A child does not expect her mother and father to have identical standards. As long as a separated or divorced couple communicate with each other about their child's experiences in either home and remain neutral in the presence of the child regarding the differences that drove them apart, she should thrive in both households.

Your home in context

In planning your youngster's room or play space, take a look at how his home environment fits into the larger environment. Think about conditions outside the home. Does he have plenty of opportunities for active outdoor play? Or do you live where these are limited? The answers should help determine how you go about designing your youngster's space.

Moving to a new home or remodeling

As your family grows, the need for additional room may arise. If you make moving plans, remember that leaving behind a familiar room can sometimes unsettle a child. You can make it easier by involving her in the move. Explain what the new place will look like and what will happen on moving day; you may wish to read her some of the books especially written to ease the transition, such as *Sad Day, Glad Day* by Vivian L. Thompson or *Moving* by Fred Rogers. Take her to the new house beforehand, if possible, and visit a park or playground in the new neighborhood. Barring this, describe her room to her and tell her what the new setting will be like. On moving day, let her help pack her toys and help you prepare her new room once the movers have unloaded your possessions.

If you plan to remodel your present home, rather than buy or rent another, talk with your child about that, too. After all, she may be moving to a new room, or you may plan to shift her toys into a new playroom. At the very least, she will be seeing a big change in her home and she deserves to be told about it beforehand so she has time to adjust.

Finding the money to remodel

Creating a new living space inevitably takes quite a bit of money. Building an extra room onto your home, or converting an attic or basement into a secure and comfortable bedroom or play area, represents a major investment. The cost of basic materials alone will be substantial. As part of your planning, you will want to consider financing options.

If you are fortunate enough to have accumulated sufficient equity in your home or if your property has risen quickly in value, you can use it to finance remodeling costs by taking out a second mortgage or opening a home equity credit line with

Moving to a New Home

❝ We made trips over to the new house with our two girls and watched it being built. When it got closer to being finished, we let the girls go in and choose their own rooms. They had few qualms about moving, and they're wonderfully attached to the house now. ❞

❝ Before school started, I arranged for the school bus to pick up our son at the new house, even though we hadn't moved in. I would drive over and wait with him until the bus came. That way he slowly got used to the neighborhood and the bus route. By the time we moved, he wasn't the new boy anymore, and he really felt at home. ❞

❝ I had prepped the mover about where to put things before we left for our new home, but I let my daughter have a hand in it, too. So when we got there, she went into her room and said, 'I want this toy here,' and 'I want my bed there.' She felt so important. ❞

❝ Being in the military, we had our belongings packed by the movers. But we made sure that Brian understood that they weren't taking his toys away forever. And we let him pack his own bag to take to the new house. He picked out everything himself, and of course he put in his favorite blanket and stuffed animal. We just kept reassuring him that all his other things would be at the new house. How happy he was to see them when we got there! ❞

❝ Moving day was wonderful. I took Megan and Katie with me to meet the mover at the unit where our things were stored, and they watched their boxes get loaded onto the truck. After not seeing their toys and furniture for six months, they had even forgotten they had a play set. Three-year-old Katie was amazed it was there—it had been *found.* ❞

❝ When we moved from one coast to the other, I thought my two little boys handled it well. But after a week they started saying that they wanted to go home. I sat down with them and we talked about how they felt. I told them that they were unhappy because they didn't have any friends yet. And then I told them that they were homesick and that they soon wouldn't be. The reassurance helped and they liked having a word to describe their feeling. ❞

❝ We let our little girl unpack her own boxes. She loved it. Everything was brand-new—everything. It was like Christmas again. We left her in her room and she played for hours. She was so happy to see her things again. ❞

❝ Before we moved in, I took the girls to a wallpaper store and handed them wallpaper books to look at. We borrowed the books and took them to the new house and held samples to the walls. They could imagine how their rooms would look. And then I did the same thing with furniture, trying to keep them involved in the whole process. ❞

a bank. As a general rule, second mortgage interest rates are usually fixed, while rates on home equity credit lines fluctuate, often with the nation's prime interest rate. The amount you can borrow is based on your equity, the appraised value of your home minus the amount you owe on your mortgage. Although this route offers certain tax advantages, you should think about it carefully. Delinquent payments could conceivably result in foreclosure. In addition, with an adjustable rate loan, you could find yourself with heavy interest payments should inflation or interest rates swell.

Refinancing your mortgage—in other words, taking out a larger mortgage loan that pays off the balance owed on your current mortgage and leaves you additional money to cover remodeling costs—is an especially attractive option if interest rates are significantly lower than they happened to be at the time you bought your home.

You may also be able to borrow against a whole life insurance policy or a company pension plan at attractive interest rates to cover your building or remodeling expenses. For younger couples who lack home equity or large insurance policies, there are numerous personal loan and home improvement loan plans available through banks, credit unions, finance companies, and other institutions. If you hire professionals for your building or remodeling job, the contractor who does the work may offer to finance the construction project, especially if you are a good credit risk but cannot qualify for other types of financing. You would be wise, however, to shop around for financing first; you may find that a lower interest rate and better payment schedule are available elsewhere.

Calling on professionals

For many jobs, it may be best to bring in experts. Working with architects, interior designers, and building contractors can be a satisfying and mostly worry-free experience if you establish a clear working relationship with the professionals who are helping you carry out your design plans.

When it comes to hiring an architect to design a new space or an interior designer to refurbish an existing one, rely on personal recommendations from friends, neighbors, and associates. Interview several and look at their portfolios to see whether their work appeals to your taste. Ask for references, and try to visit some of their clients and inspect the finished projects. Base your hiring decision on the quality of the work and your ability to communicate easily with the person chosen about your needs and ideas.

A good interior designer will want to know how the room fits into the larger context of your house, and how the building or remodeling plan fits into your budget. Be prepared to supply general information about your family's lifestyle and how you plan to use the new space, as well as such specifics as your color and style preferences and the amount of storage space you need in the room. To make your desires clear, clip out magazine and catalog pictures of schemes you admire and talk with the designer about them.

Everything in writing

The designer you choose should draw up a contract or proposal describing the job and the payment terms. You may pay a flat fee, an hourly rate, a percentage of the total construction job price, or a designer's markup on furnishings and other items. Make a point of knowing not only exactly how much the professional will charge you, but also what you are getting for your money. The designer should give you a detailed project description and cost outline or summary; read both of these items carefully and question any details that are not clear to you. Be sure that your wishes are spelled out before you sign any contract, but do not automatically assume that the job will come out just the way you envisioned it—various realities are bound to intervene along the way.

Working with a contractor

Some designers prefer to work with particular contractors, while others will suggest that you select the contractor. If the choice is up to you, follow the previously discussed procedure for hiring an interior designer or architect. Find out whether the contractor is bonded and carries workmen's compensation and liability insurance, so that you will not be financially liable for any injuries that might happen on your property. Check with the Better Business Bureau about the contractor's track record. Specify the materials to be used for the job—including brands you desire—and solicit detailed bids from several contractors. Do not let price alone be the deciding factor when choosing a contractor. A high price does not always mean high quality, while a significantly lower price may mean that the contractor will cut corners and compromise the quality of the work. You should take into consideration a contractor's reputation and experience as well as his bid.

Your contract with the builder should cover every detail of the job and specify exactly what you both have agreed on. For your legal protection, have the completion date in writing, accompanied by the words "time is of the essence," and insist on a contractual guarantee that the job will be performed "in a workmanlike manner." Many people pay the builder a third of the fee upon signing the contract, another third at some point during the job, and the final third when everything has been finished to satisfaction.

Inspect the work frequently and insist that it adhere to your specifications. Any changes made along the way should be put in writing, with new written cost statements from the contractor. At the job's completion, carry out a close inspection and make a written list of any finishing touches still required. Make your final payment only after the contractor has taken care of every last detail on your list. ❖

Redesigning Space to Suit Your Child

Your young one needs a living space that suits him—indeed, fits him—and in planning his room or play area you will want to take into account the fact that he will be developing and growing all the while. Creating an appropriate and adaptable room may seem like a big chore, but all that is really necessary are some forethought and some simple design tools, including planning the room on paper before actually decorating it. Trying out your ideas in advance can save both energy and money later and eliminate mistakes you and your child might otherwise have to live with for a long time to come.

The basic design principles discussed on the following pages offer ways of using best the features that are already present in the room. Floors, walls, ceiling, windows, and lighting are all to be considered; understanding their possibilities will make the job of organizing and using the available space to ultimate advantage easier.

Whatever choices you make, you should remember to provide enough leeway for your child to strike out on his own and to exploit fully the potential of the room and its furnishings. And again, whenever you can, include him in the decisions. Experts say such participation gives a child a feeling of pride and encourages a more responsible attitude toward his home environment and possessions.

Designing for scale Even after your child outgrows booster seats and highchairs, he still has a need for furniture and space that reflect his size. Tables that are too high or drawers and shelves that are tantalizingly out of reach present barriers to his sense of mastery. By scaling down furnishings and taking into account the accessibility of various items, you will be giving him the opportunity to exercise some control over his environment. Buy juvenile furniture, or secondhand pieces whose legs can be shortened by several inches. Install hooks and clothes racks where your youngster can reach them; let him have the satisfaction of switches and lighting fixtures that he can readily turn on and off.

With all his possessions immediately at hand, he will find it easier to perform such tasks as dressing himself, putting away toys, and hanging up clothes. And then as he adds inches to his height, adjust the room's features to reflect his elevated view of the world. For example, you can hang clothes racks higher in his closet and adjust the level of the shelves on which he stores his belongings. Such accommodations will do much to help him keep things in order and relieve you of some of the burden of having to pick up after him.

In designing your child's room, take into account her various play and sleeping requirements as well as her future growth. A large, open space is ideal for some children's activities, but your youngster will probably also like having small, enclosed spaces to snuggle in. With a large room, you can arrange the furniture to break up the space into smaller, cozier units, or you can use partitions to create nooks and cubbies.

Providing your child with a feeling of security in her sleeping area is also important. Listen to what she says about her fears and pay attention to her fantasies. Avoid a bed that is too large for her and think twice about its position; you certainly do not want her to feel stranded in the middle of an emptiness. Position a crib or bed close to one or two walls for snugness. In many homes, of course, the problem is just the opposite—too little space. There are ways, happily, of addressing it. If your child has a small room, you can make it seem larger by creative decorating and intelligent use of all available space. For an open and uncluttered look, keep the furniture to a minimum. Select small, low pieces and arrange them against the walls to free up the center of the room. Eliminate extra accessories, such as too many pictures breaking up an expanse of wall, and use simple window treatments to prevent a heavy look that can make the room seem less open. Buy multipurpose furniture, such as a bed with shelves and storage compartments built into the headboard. Save

Fooling the Eye to Advantage

You cannot actually make a small room larger without major construction, but there are ways to make it seem bigger than it is. A few imaginative and relatively inexpensive touches can visually enlarge a room, enhancing even the tightest space.

One way to do this is with mirrors. Strategically placed to reflect window views or elements of room décor, properly chosen mirrors will contribute a welcome feeling of spaciousness. You can draw the eye into a seemingly infinite series of reflections by positioning two mirrors to reflect each other, for example. You can also buy mirror squares, with adhesive backs, and affix

these to the wall. If you use hanging mirrors, try to keep them out of your child's reach, and make sure to use picture wire and hooks strong enough to support the weight. With a large mirror, you may want to obtain the services of a professional picture hanger for maximum safety.

Painting techniques can also seem to open up a room. You can use a fanciful optical illusion *(opposite, top)* to create a "hole" in the wall that will fascinate your youngster. But if you lack the artist's touch, the easy trick shown opposite, bottom, will serve you just as well.

Positioned in a corner of a child's room, at right angles to the bookcase, this wall mirror appears to extend the shelving and richly multiplies the shapes and colors of books, toys, and other belongings. The mirror has the further advantage of reflecting light back into the room.

This simple trompe l'oeil (literally, "fools the eye")
painting of a cat and a potted plant will tease and
mystify a young child, who may puzzle over such a
mysterious three-dimensional "hole" in the wall. The
painting opens up a small room by drawing the eye out
through the illusory window.

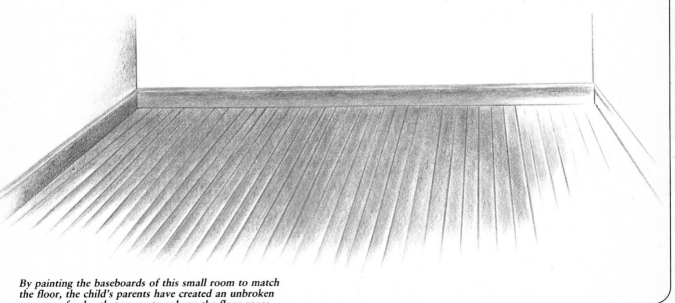

By painting the baseboards of this small room to match
the floor, the child's parents have created an unbroken
expanse of color that seems to enlarge the floor space.
You can extend this illusion overhead by bringing the
color of the ceiling a few inches down the walls.

floor space by using wall-hung shelves rather than standing cabinets or bookcases; furniture that can be folded or hidden away—folding chairs or trundle beds, for instance—will also conserve precious play space. Paint the walls with light colors and use simple, unobtrusive patterns for draperies and bedspreads. Create a feeling of greater height in a room with a low ceiling by drawing the eye up to an attractive toy or stuffed animal placed on top of an armoire or a high bookcase. To brighten and enlarge a dark room, consider adding a skylight or an extra window. (For more decorating ideas, see pages 20-21.)

Developing a plan
A child's room needs at least one major focal point—the center of activity. It may also include several distinct areas for different kinds of play. To find the best possible use of the available space, first draw up a floor plan; besides providing a handy bird's-eye view of the room, it allows you to experiment on paper with various furniture groupings. A floor plan will also identify any problems that can be solved through visual illusion, color, or other sleight-of-hand design schemes. After making a scale drawing, you may discover that you have more strategies for maximizing your child's space than you originally thought. Additionally, the drawing will save you the trouble of shifting heavy pieces of furniture around until they fit. For help with this useful mapping process, see the box opposite.

As you experiment with pencil-sketch or template furniture arrangements—scale cutouts you can make—keep in mind that doors and windows should remain accessible, for safety, ventilation, and ease of movement. Since doors do much to control the traffic flow in and out of a room, allow a two-foot-wide traffic lane for any likely paths through the room. Penciling these in on your floor plan will help you plot play areas; otherwise your youngster and his friends will be stepping in and out of one another's truck routes or knocking over building-block constructions. Also make sure that desk and dresser have enough space in front of them for drawers to be opened conveniently. Allow plenty of room for multipurpose or special furniture—rocking space for a rocking chair and foldout space for a convertible couch, for example. Remember, too, that you will need to leave room for sliding out a desk chair or pulling a bed out from the wall to make it.

When you have everything arranged the way you like it in your scale drawing, go one step further and cut out life-size furniture templates from newspaper or brown wrapping paper. Arrange these according to your plan and give yourself a day or

Planning Your Youngster's Room on Paper

Before setting up your child's room, you can save yourself a lot of trouble and mistakes by working it all out on paper. The cutouts arrayed on the graph-paper grid below show one possible arrangement of a baby's nursery, containing a changing table, laundry hamper, and crib, as well as a bookcase, dresser, and rocking chair.

Start by taking careful measurements of the room's length, width, and height. Then choose a scale for your drawing; here two squares stand for one foot. Using your measurements, map the room on graph paper. The measurements will come in handy later when you order wallpaper, paint, or carpeting.

Determine the positions and sizes of windows, doorways, electrical outlets, and radiators or vents, as well as any alcoves or odd corners, and add them to your drawing. Also note any sloping walls or overhead beams; these will dictate the height of the furniture you can use in those parts of the room.

When your scale drawing is complete, measure the furniture you plan to use in the room and convert those measurements to the grid scale. You can then cut out paper templates to represent the furniture and shift them around, or you can sketch the furniture on the paper and try new arrangements by erasing and resketching. Still another method is to trace several schemes on tissue-paper overlays. The reward of creating a plan is gaining a sense of not only how the room will look, but also of how it will work, enabling you to avoid obstructing vents or radiators and having doors swing open onto furniture.

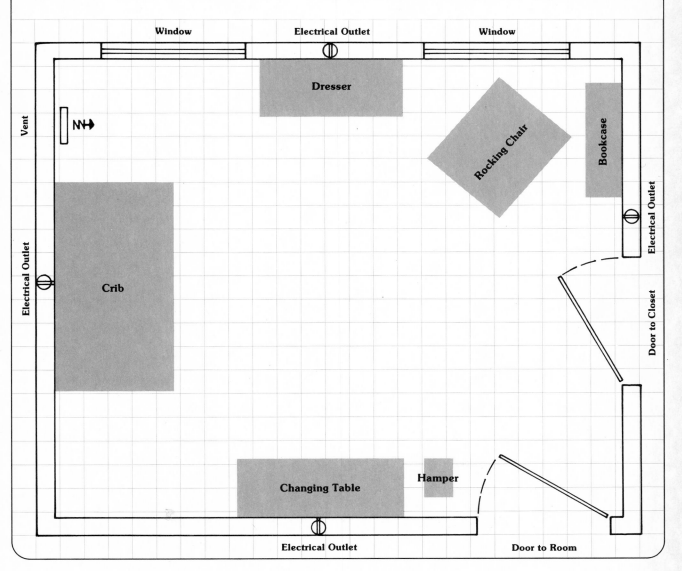

two to see whether you still feel comfortable with the layout. With life-size templates, you may discover something you did not see on the smaller scale, such as the necessity of having to bend over a dresser to open a window. In lieu of paper cutouts, you can mark off areas with masking tape.

The anatomy of color   One of the most fundamental elements of room design, and one that will profoundly influence the look and feel of your child's room, is color. If possible, take your youngster to paint, wallpaper, fabric, or carpet stores to collect color samples. Sit down with him and play mix-and-match games to select the best combinations; give him several choices, being careful not to overwhelm him with too many alternatives. Trust your own taste, but keep in mind that the subtle, muted hues that you prefer may not satisfy his craving for bright, bold colors. If your child's taste runs to some particularly garish color, perhaps you can indulge him by painting one section of wall his choice or using it for accessories.

In choosing among the innumerable colors available, you will be aided if you know the language of color. When decorators talk about hue, they are using a synonym for color, the quality that enables us to distinguish green from red, yellow from purple, and so on. Saturation, which is also called chroma or intensity, refers to the strength, richness, or purity of a color. The green of grass is more saturated than the green of lime juice. Value is the term for a color's lightness or darkness. Navy blue and robin's-egg blue are variations on the same color, but they have very different values. Navy blue is a shade, created by adding black to a color, while robin's-egg blue is a tint, which is made by mixing in white.

Colors are sometimes described in terms of their temperature. Certain hues, such as red, orange, and yellow, are said to be warm. Others, such as blue, green, and purple, are referred to as cool. Studies have shown that color temperature can have psychological and even physical effects on us. Warm colors are jazzy and stimulating, while cool colors are soothing and relaxing. Red tends to raise blood pressure and pulse rate, blue to lower them. The concept of color temperature also applies to the many kinds of off-white that can be created by mixing pure white with minute amounts of other colors. If you choose off-white as part of the color scheme for your youngster's room, be sensitive to the temperature differences between, for example, one off-white that leans toward a warm yellow and another one that hints of blue.

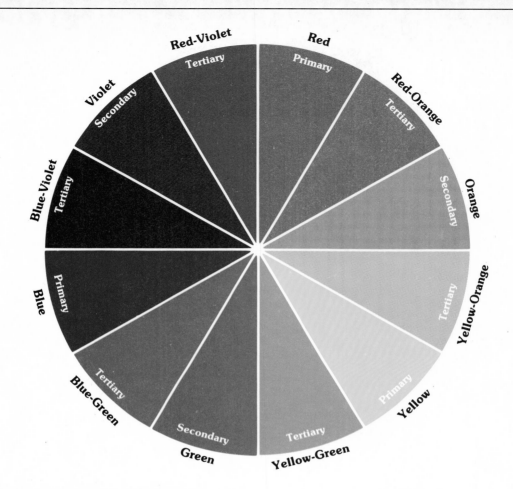

The color wheel labels, arranged clockwise: Red (Primary), Red-Orange (Tertiary), Orange (Secondary), Yellow-Orange (Tertiary), Yellow (Primary), Yellow-Green (Tertiary), Green (Secondary), Blue-Green (Tertiary), Blue (Primary), Blue-Violet (Tertiary), Violet (Secondary), Red-Violet (Tertiary)

The Wonderful Color Wheel

Picking colors for your child's room becomes easier when you understand something about them. A color wheel is a handy guide, showing you how to achieve pleasing combinations of complementary and contrasting hues. It works this way:

The primary colors, at equidistant points on the wheel, constitute the colors from which all other colors are derived: blue, red, and yellow. Every other color in the spectrum is a mixture of these in varying proportions.

The secondary colors are made of two primaries mixed in equal proportions. Orange is a blend of yellow and red; purple, or violet, is made of red and blue; and green is a combination of blue and yellow.

The tertiary colors are an equal blend of a secondary and one of its two adjacent primaries. Combining secondary and primary colors results in yellow-green, red-orange, and blue-violet, as well as blue-green, yellow-orange, and red-violet.

Beyond primary, secondary, and tertiary colors, an infinite variety of other hues derives from more complex combinations and proportions. For instance, instead of mixing equal amounts of blue and red to form violet, a greater proportion of blue to red creates a rich plum purple, while more red than blue results in a reddish wine color. Other combinations might involve mixing a tertiary color with a primary color or with a secondary color.

White and black are not regarded as actual colors, and therefore they do not appear on the color wheel. Neither do the so-called neutrals—gray, which is made by mixing black and white or by mixing the primary colors equally, or brown, which is an unequal combination of the primary colors. These hues, too, can be blended in different combinations ranging, for example, from pale beige to deep chocolate brown, or from light gray to dark charcoal gray. Often used for walls and floors, neutrals can create the illusion of expanded space and help accentuate brighter colors.

Color's Transforming Magic

Coming up with a pleasing and well-balanced color scheme for your child's room is easier than you may think. Keeping her favorite hues in mind, you can experiment with three tried-and-true approaches represented below and on the next page—referred to as complementary, analogous (or related), and triadic—before deciding on the combination that most pleases you and your youngster.

A successful color scheme requires that you not only balance colors, but also distribute them well. Decide first on a dominant color; then limit your scheme to several colors and give companion hues a secondary role to keep the various components from competing. Consider also using neutrals for floor and walls.

Some parents find it easiest to use a light hue for walls and floor coverings and then to accent it with more intense hues in accessories or small prints. Equally simple is to choose one color for furnishings, window coverings, and walls and to use another for the floor, with accessories picking up both colors and possibly providing another color for spice. The sample rooms on these pages show how paint, carpet, and fabric colors, along with accessories, can be mixed and matched for a professional, pulled-together look.

For success without much guesswork, consider also a monochromatic color scheme, not pictured here. This involves using one color in its many rich intensities, from light to dark, but requires that you vary the patterns and textures in the room for maximum visual interest.

Your own color choices will very likely differ from the examples given on these pages, but the guiding principles remain the same. Use the color wheel on the previous page for guidance, and be sure to let your child's imagination play a role, too.

Complementary color scheme

This child's room incorporates subtle variations of the complementary colors red and green. The rosy pink of the pillow sham and the pale pink walls contrast with the muted green rug; these are accented by white. For a complementary scheme, work with colors opposite each other on the color wheel.

Analogous color scheme

Here, light blue, royal blue, and green blend peacefully. The light blue wall paint and the royal blue curtains and bedspread lend richness. The green rug with white accents, the lamp, and picture catch secondary hues in the fabrics for a bright touch. For an analogous scheme, pick three or four neighboring hues on the color wheel.

Triadic color scheme

The splashy colors of this room have a unified, lively appeal; the happy yellow hues of the bedspread and curtains vividly counterpoint the rug's vibrant red. The white and blue accessories echo the same hues in the fabrics and rug. For a triadic scheme, you must work with equidistant colors on the color wheel.

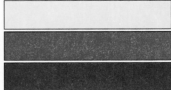

Choosing and using color

When selecting colors for your child's room, keep in mind their potential for helping you solve some thorny design problems. For example, color can have a powerful effect on space. Light walls tend to recede, enlarging the room for an open, spacious impression, while dark walls have just the opposite effect, shrinking the room for a cozier space. But take care in deciding how much of each color to use, especially vivid colors, since by their very nature they will tend to dominate.

Remember also that colors seem to change when placed next to each other. Light colors appear lighter beside contrasting dark colors, while white increases the power of adjacent colors. Paint of the same color will look different on walls of different textures, since rough surfaces tend to absorb light and cast shadows, and smooth, glossy surfaces to reflect light. A color can also change according to lighting conditions. You should always bring color samples home to examine in the room itself, under natural and artificial light, at different times of the day, and in different combinations.

A floor your child can use

Your child's floor will probably be the most used part of her room. Because of her size, she is much closer to the floor than you are. She crawls on it, walks, lies down, and plops on it. She rolls wheeled toys across it, and she often uses it in preference to a desk or tabletop for such activities as drawing or board games. A surface that figures so prominently in your youngster's life—not just in her room, of course, but throughout the house—deserves some special attention.

From a practical standpoint, the floor should be easy to keep clean, safe to play on, and adaptable. It should be flat and smooth so that a child can play with blocks and other toys. It should also be warm, not too slippery, as soundproof as possible, tough enough to take the heavy punishment she and her friends are bound to give it, yet resilient enough to cushion the inevitable falls. No one type of floor meets all of these requirements, but you can pick among the many kinds available to provide a floor surface that is right for your child.

Choosing between hard and soft surfaces

A durable, resilient surface, such as vinyl or wood, is easier to keep clean than carpeting and is appropriate for blocks, wheeled toys, and pursuits involving paint, glue, or modeling clay. Carpeting, on the other hand, is warmer, more sound absorbent, and more comfortable for very young children who are crawling or taking frequent tumbles as they learn to walk.

There are a number of floor design strategies you can adopt

to give your child the best of both worlds—the flatness and washability of a hard surface and the soft, quiet insulation of carpeting. You can carpet the entire room, for example, then use mats—vinyl, rubber, or the kind of hard plastic placed under wheeled office chairs—on areas where they will be needed. Gym mats offer another possibility; they can be rolled up and stored when not in use. Some parents have found that carpeting half the room and providing a hard surface for the other half is a perfect compromise. Another solution is to spread area rugs with nonslip backing in appropriate sections of the room. Then again you might consider picking synthetic fiber carpeting with a very low pile and covering the entire floor with it, gaining a surface almost as flat and smooth as wood or vinyl.

Carpeting is available in a tremendous range of colors, patterns, and fibers, but your choice may be somewhat restricted by intended use. Deep-pile shag carpeting is impractical in a child's room, since it is difficult to keep clean. A low cut-pile or short-loop, dense-weave carpet is a better choice, preventing tiny objects or game pieces from becoming concealed in the fibers. In addition, a dense carpet wears well, outlasting skimpier ones. A wool rug is hard to clean even when it has a low pile, and wool may cause allergic reactions, although it is attractive and durable. Many nonallergenic artificial fibers, including nylon, acrylic, polyester, and olefin, are less expensive than wool and easier to maintain; indeed, many are treated with stain repellents. If you live in a dry climate, check that the carpet you choose has been treated to avoid static buildup. Likewise, in a damp climate, look for a mildew-resistant carpet. All synthetics are mildew-proof,

A small area rug lures a child with its snuggly teddy bear pattern. The carpet has a nonslip backing for safety. The hard flooring around the rug provides ample space for active play.

and wool can be treated to resist mildew. In making your choice, remember that medium-value colors show dirt less than extremely dark or light hues. Some parents find carpet tiles a sensible way to cover a child's floor; if one section is stained, or worn, it can be instantly replaced.

When shopping for carpeting, always find out whether the price includes padding and installation. A pad makes the carpet feel softer, adds another layer of sound-proofing, improves appearance, and helps reduce wear. Check to be certain that the carpet padding is a nonallergenic, synthetic material.

While not as soft and warm as carpeting, sealed wood flooring and vinyl coverings are extremely easy to clean and can be very attractive. Vinyl is resilient and comfortable underfoot, and it comes in diverse patterns and textures. Wood floors can be treated in a number of ways, depending on the look you want. You can stain them, paint them in solid colors, or stencil on multicolored designs. If you leave your child's wood floor un-carpeted, you should go over it first to see that it has been well sanded and that it is free of splinters before sealing it with several coats of hardwearing polyurethane.

From the time your child can focus her eyes, you will notice her curiously gazing at the walls and ceilings. They define the outer borders of her world; they also envelop her in security and, when she is old enough to need it, provide her with some privacy. Ceilings, as well as walls, offer you the opportunity to create a stimulating environment for your child. To make a ceiling visually exciting, paint on designs or apply stick-on cutouts. When it comes to walls, your options, of course, are wider still. Paint, wallpaper, paneling, and other coverings give you a range of options, each

A girl reaches toward the canopy of heavenly bodies that decorate her wall and ceiling. You can cut out simple star, moon, and sun patterns like those above and opposite from adhesive paper. Look for a brand that peels off easily.

one with its own advantages and disadvantages.

Paint is inexpensive, you can apply it yourself, and since there is virtually no limit on color selection, you can easily match it to fabrics, carpeting, and the various accessories you have picked out to accent the room. And when your youngster matures and grows tired of her childhood color scheme, you have only to repaint the room to update it. If you are artistically inclined, you can buy stencils and several different colors of paint and apply designs, murals, or supergraphics—bright patterns that will enliven a large wall or ceiling area. You can also employ various painting techniques to enhance the walls, such as using a paint-soaked sponge to give the surface a subtle mottled look *(cover)*.

Paint for a child's room should be purchased with its washability in mind, since children inevitably leave smudges and marks on walls and woodwork. The most washable paint is high gloss, which reflects light, thus brightening a room. On the negative side, it produces glare and highlights every bump, knick, crack, and nail hole in a wall's surface. Flat, nonreflecting paints are the least washable but the best for camouflaging such flaws. Semigloss paint is a good compromise, offering a washable surface without too much sheen. If semigloss is too shiny for you, select a satin or eggshell finish. Water-base paint, or latex paint, is easier to work with than the oil-base alternatives because it spreads well, dries quickly, and scrubs clean with just soap and water. If you are fixing up a baby's nursery, air out the space thoroughly once you are done, especially if you have used oil-base paints, before settling the infant in the room.

Wallpaper is more expensive, harder to apply, and harder to replace than paint, and it gives you less flexibility in changing it. Despite these drawbacks, the right wallpaper pattern can add character and charm to a room and hide imperfections in the wall better than paint. Washable, vinyl-coated wallpaper is best

A Shade of Difference

You can dress up windows in your child's room by adding a colorful border of hand-painted figures or shapes to what otherwise would be a plain shade. For best results, use a shade with a surface as smooth as possible so that the paint will adhere; an inexpensive vinyl shade will do. Determine the exact center of the shade's bottom edge since you will want your design to be symmetrical, and work from this point outward on either side. Draw the outlines lightly in pencil. If you are not a particularly good artist, you may wish to trace around some of your child's toys, as pictured below, or use cookie cutters or household objects. With the outlines done, you have only to fill them in with paint and add any details you like.

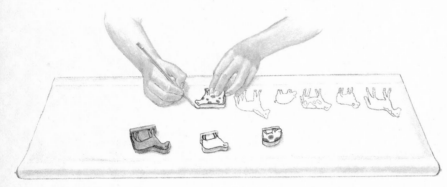

1

To make a border like the one pictured above, position toy animals or any other figures that please you one by one along the shade's edge and then draw around them with pencil. Some one-dimensional animal toys have painted-on legs; if so, pencil in the necessary lines.

2

To fill in the shapes, put several dabs of acrylic paint on a plate, along with a squirt of dish-washing detergent, which will help the paint stick to the shade. Dip your paintbrush first in a bowl of water, then in the detergent, and then in the paint. Once the paint is dry, outline the animals in indelible ink.

for a child's room. Some brands of wallpaper are prepasted for easy hanging, but most have to be spread with paste, a task that requires a fair amount of skill and patience. You might want to consider hiring a professional wallpaperer and then doing the rest of the decorating yourself.

If you would prefer not to paper the entire room yet would still like some of the cheer wallpaper provides, you can use decorative wallpaper borders instead and apply them as you like—at chair-rail height, midway up the wall, or where the walls and ceiling meet. Borders are inexpensive and can do as effective a job of individualizing a room as yards and yards of wallpaper; they can also be removed and changed with little trouble.

Paneling, fabric, and bulletin board surfaces have something to say for them if your intention is to conceal a bad wall or add some soundproofing to a room. A bulletin board wall gives a preschooler a place to display her artwork prominently, but for a young child, the board's pushpins and thumbtacks can be hazardous. Attractive though it might be on a wall, fabric gathers dust and might be pulled down by an active child. If you pick a fabric covering, attach it to the wall with interlocking plastic strips or hang it from curtain rods at the floor and ceiling so that you can take it down for laundering. Paneling is one of the most durable wall coverings, but it is also one of the most expensive, and its darker wood tones often lack the kind of brightness children respond to.

Controlling light and dressing up windows

Windows are both practical and ornamental features, and they offer many opportunities for bringing a room to life. You can cover them with curtains, shades, blinds, shutters, or combinations of these. Whichever you choose, look for materials that are easy to maintain.

Shades, available in many styles and materials, are generally inexpensive to buy. They serve an all-important function—blocking out light when you want your baby to sleep beyond the first crack of dawn or doze off at naptime. You can brighten up even the plainest roller shades with easy homemade decorations *(opposite)*. Blinds give you more control over the amount of light you let into the room, allowing you to close them completely for total darkness, angle the thin slats slightly for filtered light, or pull them up for full light. They too are relatively inexpensive, and they can be easily wiped clean. If you go with blinds, be sure to keep the cords out of a toddler's reach, as you would with any drapery cords.

Curtains can be used by themselves or in combination with

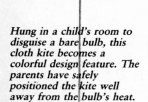

Hung in a child's room to disguise a bare bulb, this cloth kite becomes a colorful design feature. The parents have safely positioned the kite well away from the bulb's heat.

blinds or shades. You can choose the color, pattern, and texture of the material to blend in with the rest of the room décor or to provide an eye-catching contrast. Curtains are one of the simplest features of the room to change, and the wide selection on the market gives you a virtually limitless supply of new patterns and styles to choose from as your youngster grows up and develops different tastes and interests. In buying curtains, keep in mind that long ones are impractical in a young child's room, where they can be tripped over or tugged at by little hands. Window frames, too, can be painted bright colors, or you can stencil a design on the wall around a curtainless window to create a pleasing effect.

Shutters are durable and attractive but expensive, and they require time and skill to install. If you do not have the tools or the know-how but do want the finished look shutters provide, have a professional hang them for you.

Your child will need ample general lighting in his room and play area, as well as specific lighting for special activities. Some parents put up track lights or reflector spot lamps that provide overall illumination and at the same time can be angled to shed light where needed, as on a reading chair or worktable. To get some insight into your youngster's lighting needs, you should take note of how he uses his room. He may prefer, for example, to look at books on the floor, and thus good overall lighting would be in order.

In positioning a lamp or fixture, examine it from your child's level and angle of vision to make sure it will not shine in his eyes or produce a glare. Arrange to have light switches within his reach; many extenders slip right over the light switch, making it easy for children to grab them and turn the light on or off.

When it comes to buying lamps and fixtures, you have several options. Wall fixtures can be placed out of children's reach and eliminate the problem of tripping over cords. Track lighting not only gives you the flexibility of aiming the beam at various targets, but also of being able to attach extendable arms that focus illumination even more precisely. Because of its harshness, fluorescent lighting has not been used much in children's rooms, but thanks to recent advances, warmer tones are available. Whether fluorescent or incandescent, desk and table lamps will add color and interest to a room, and these are often designed with children in mind. Some have flexible arms that let you or your child direct the light. When your youngster is old enough to read in bed, you might want to hang a wall-mounted lamp over his headboard. A plastic one is less likely to injure the child if it happens to get accidentally knocked down.

Your youngster may fall asleep more happily with a night-light burning in the room. If you use a small light that plugs into a wall socket, be sure to position it so bedclothes or curtains do not fall across it. Any light connected to a dimmer can be turned down for a night-light. If you plug a lamp into a timer, you can set it and leave it burning for an hour or so after bedtime.

There are safety concerns that you should keep in mind as you plan the lighting for the room. Do not put table lamps where they can be knocked over or pulled to the floor. Keep all lamps well out of reach when your child is small, so he will not burn himself on the bulbs, and avoid metal lampshades, which can heat up quickly.

The question of heat and ventilation

Babies are born with only a modest ability to regulate their body temperature, and it is important, therefore, that their rooms be neither too hot nor too cold. In general, a baby younger than one month old or weighing less than eight pounds should have his room temperature kept at about seventy degrees Fahrenheit. Above that weight, a child has enough fat to serve as insulation, and it is safe to turn the temperature down to the low sixties, providing he is well covered. Use a baby's arms or neck as a guide to his heating needs rather than his hands; if the skin is warm, he is too. Many new parents overdress a new baby and overheat the home environment and then continue to do so even when the child is older. A sensible approach is to keep your youngster out of drafts and to be careful not to let the room become too warm, which can be just as uncomfortable as an icy atmosphere.

In the wintertime, the heat in your home is likely to dry out the mucous membranes in your child's nose and mouth and rob his skin of moisture. Since a lower resistance to germs may result from dryness of the nose and mouth, you may choose to use a cool-mist humidifier in his room. Keep the humidifier scrupulously clean so it will not spread germs and molds, and empty it when it is not in use to prevent microorganisms from breeding in any standing water.

Maintenance

You can simplify the job of cleaning your child's room or playroom by making sensible choices. The fabrics for curtains, bedspreads, wall hangings, or any other purpose should be washable or responsive to chemical spot cleaners *(box, page 37)*. Walls, shelves, tabletops, woodwork, and other surfaces should be easy to wipe clean. If your child has pets, keep in mind that a fishtank or hamster cage will inevitably produce a messy area in need of regular policing. Similarly, a blackboard hung on the wall will leave chalk dust on the floor beneath it, so you will want to hang it over flooring that can be easily cleaned.

How often you clean a carpet depends on how much dirt it picks up, which depends in turn on such factors as how often your child uses the room, how many playmates use it with him, and what sort of activities take place there. In general, you should vacuum a carpet at least once or twice a week for longest wear. If anything spills on the carpet, clean it up immediately, and have the carpet professionally cleaned from time to time to keep it in the best possible condition. You may want to conserve the carpet further by occasionally rearranging the furniture in the room. This will prevent the pile from denting permanently, as well as developing wear patterns. You can protect area rugs against uneven wear by turning them periodically.

You should never use any cleaning product without first reading the instructions on the container. Since you will need them for reference, always save manufacturer's instructions for cleaning wall coverings, flooring, or fabrics, and file these where you can get at them when needed. If you are not sure about how well a particular cleaner works, test it on some small, inconspicuous spot before using it for a major cleaning job.

Be aware that you or your child may be allergic to some of the chemicals contained in certain household cleaners. Before you let your youngster play where one has been used, check to see that the area is dry and free of fumes. You should be able to clean fingerprints and other dirt from most washable surfaces with a mild solution of detergent and water. A soft mop or cloth will suffice for dust. Use a damp mop on vinyl floors or polyurethaned wood, and a damp sponge or cloth on paint, wallpaper, shades, and blinds. And for sanity's sake, you had better resign yourself to the fact that your child's room or play space, by the very nature of its use, will always be a little messy, no matter how hard you work to keep it neat and clean.

Your life will be a whole lot easier if you establish some rules as to where certain activities are carried on. By insisting that all snacking take place in the kitchen, you will be saving yourself the trouble of having to sweep up crumbs or mop up spilled drinks elsewhere in the house. Similarly, you may restrict something as rewarding but messy as mixing modeling dough to the kitchen table. In imposing such limitations, you will not only be sparing yourself aggravation, but also teaching your child something about responsibility. ❖

How to Remove Stains from Washables

Armed with a handful of home laundry products, you can remove almost any stain from washable fabric. You will need an enzyme laundry detergent, household ammonia, white vinegar, a prewash product for loosening dirt, oxygen bleach and chlorine bleach, and a dry-cleaning solvent, all found in grocery or hardware stores. You should also have on hand several absorbent white cloths and soft-bristled nylon brushes.

Stains are best removed if attended to immediately. This is particularly true of water-soluble stains, which are easiest to remove when treated with water right away. Still, in the case of most stains, success requires patience, gentleness, and perhaps the repetition of a procedure. Avoid weakening a fabric with hard scrubbing, and always test a treatment on an inconspicuous spot, such as the inside of a seam or hem, to see whether the fabric will be harmed.

You may want to add a bleach to the wash water when laundering a garment after stain-removal treatment. Oxygen bleach is safe for all fabrics and colors. Chlorine bleach cannot be used on silk, wool, spandex, noncolorfast fabrics, or certain flame-retardant fabrics.

Be aware that cleaning agents can be hazardous. Never mix ammonia and chlorine bleach; toxic fumes will result. Store and use cleaning fluids only in well-ventilated areas, away from flames or pilot lights, since many are flammable. Wear goggles and rubber gloves and avoid inhaling fumes, which can burn skin and eyes. Never use a second cleaning agent without rinsing out the first. Hang soaked rags outside to dry and wash them before storing them.

This chart lists the best methods for removing common childhood stains. Most stains are oily, albuminous, or tannic; each has its own cleaning method, described below. When you have a stain to remove, check the list at the bottom of this page. It will either refer you to one of the three methods or give a specific treatment.

Method 1

Oily, greasy stains. These are best removed, especially if in a heavy concentration, by flushing the area with a dry-cleaning solvent followed by air-drying, spraying with a prewash spray, and washing.

Method 2

Albuminous stains. Protein-based stains; milk or dairy by-products; many foods; blood and body discharges. Best removed with a slightly alkaline solution. Combine 2 tablespoons of household ammonia and 1 tablespoon of laundry detergent in a cup of warm water; brush this into the stain and wash.

Method 3

Tannic stains. Fruit juices; mixed drinks; and beverages containing tannin, such as tea. Best taken out with slightly acid spot remover. Mix 2 tablespoons of white vinegar and 1 tablespoon of laundry detergent into one cup of warm water; brush this solution into the stain and wash the fabric thoroughly.

Directory of Stains

Baby oil, baby cream: Method 1

Blood: Rinse stain with cold water. Make a spot remover of 2 tablespoons of household ammonia in a cup of cool water to which 1 tablespoon of an enzyme detergent is added. Brush this solution into the stain and wash.

Candy: Method 3

Chewing gum: One method of removing gum is to wrap an ice cube in a plastic bag and hold it against the gum until the entire wad is brittle. Then use the edge of a stainless-steel spoon to pry the chewing gum off. If the gum sticks, rap it sharply with the spoon's edge and chip it away in pieces. Another tactic for removal is to sponge the chewing gum with a dry-cleaning fluid; rinse and, if necessary, launder in hottest water that the fabric will permit.

Chocolate: Method 2

Cough syrup: Method 2

Crayon: Method 1

Feces: Method 2

Finger paint, watercolor paint: If still wet, wash out with laundry detergent and water. With dried stains, place the stained area on a solid surface, apply a dry-cleaning solvent and tap the stain gently with the tips of the bristles of a soft brush to break it up. Repeat until no further stain removal occurs. Flush with solvent and let dry. Then saturate the area with a spray prewash product, again tap with the brush to break up any remaining stain, and launder.

Formula: Method 2

Fruit, fruit juice: Method 3

Grass: Method 2

Grease: Method 1

Ice cream: Method 2

Ink: Put paper towels or a clean white rag under the fabric. Blot the area well with dry-cleaning solvent until no more ink bleeds into the paper or rag used.

Flush the area with solvent and let air-dry. Then saturate with an acid spotting solution (*Method 3, above*) and launder.

Jam, jelly: Method 3

Ketchup: Method 3

Milk: Method 2

Mucus: Method 2

Mud: Method 2

Mustard: Method 3

Pencil: Sponge with dry-cleaning fluid, rinse; if necessary, launder using hottest water fabric will stand.

Petroleum jelly: Method 1

Soft drinks: Method 3

Urine: Method 2

Vegetables: Method 3

Vomit: Method 2

Room for Growth

More than just a place to sleep and change clothes, your child's room can contribute significantly to his overall development as a human being. Indeed, not only can you set it up in a way that will nurture his emerging abilities and independence, but you can also decorate it in a manner that will reflect his personality and interests. Since he will grow dramatically in the years ahead, you will want to design a room that will grow with him as well.

The bedroom pictured opposite reflects the young inhabitant's passion for boats—through the nautical print over his bed, the model sailboat on the shelf, and the cheerful border of ships his mother has stenciled on the walls. Yet all of these decorative features—even the stenciling—can swiftly be replaced with other more appropriate elements as the youngster's interests change. The storage units, which offer both open and concealed spaces, will be useful throughout his childhood, but his toddler-size bed will presently give way to a larger one.

The pages that follow suggest ways you can keep the furnishings and décor of your child's room flexible and easily adapt the room to his needs at each stage of childhood—from infancy through toddlerhood and on through the preschool years. Perhaps you will decide to have siblings share a room. This chapter also offers various arrangements you can use to give roommates the best chances for getting along well together and expressing their individuality at the same time.

A Nest for Baby

Whether you are about to have your first baby, your second, or even your third, setting up a nursery especially for the new arrival is a task to enjoy. Indeed, choosing a cradle or crib, deciding where to put it, and imagining the tiny newborn comfortably settled in are preoccupations that can help fill the last months of waiting for the birth with special pleasure. All the same, it is not unusual to feel some dismay at the prospect of giving up precious living space and probably having to redo the room as well—and it is wise therefore to address these concerns through careful planning. Start by considering the special needs of a newborn, remembering that babies grow and change quickly. You will probably end up adapting the nursery during the first months of your child's life, as her personality develops and her requirements change. Give thought also to your own needs in caring for an infant, as well as the needs of other family members. Keep infant safety in mind, too. And while practical considerations must come first, permit yourself the fun of buying or making some dream items, too.

Locating the nursery

One decision you will have to make early in your planning is where to locate the nursery. Understanding what a small baby needs from his surroundings can help you choose an appropriate room. A newborn demands lots of love and attention, but in terms of accommodations, his requirements are modest. He should be given a comfortable but relatively small space in which to slumber away the hours—one neither too cool nor too warm, where there is fresh air, and windows to let in the sun. He does not need total quiet to sleep—quite the contrary, in fact. If he gets used to silence, he may startle and awaken at the slightest sound. So, while you naturally will not want to put him to bed near a blaring radio or a noisy workshop, you should know that most babies are capable of sleeping through the murmur of conversation or the sounds of dinner preparations.

You will do well also to keep your own convenience in mind when you choose a nursery space. As veteran parents recognize from experience, tending to a newborn is demanding: No sooner have you changed a diaper than it is wet again. This is a good reason to situate the nursery near a bathroom. And if you are bottle-feeding your infant, consider the length of your midnight treks to the kitchen. Personal needs are still another factor. It may be impractical for a parent to surrender a study or home office, and it would be unwise to displace a toddler who is already unhappy about sharing his parents with a baby.

As you can see, there are guidelines to help you in setting up a nursery, but no rigid rules. In fact, in a small house or apartment, where space is at a premium, you may not want to give over an entire room, at least not at first. Your baby's nursery might be one end of the living room, a corner of the dining room, even a large, well-ventilated walk-in closet, perhaps with a window. A screen or curtain will make the improvised nursery more private, and you can decorate it with a few appropriate items.

Sharing your room

During the early months, an infant can sleep quite comfortably in your room. Many parents, especially first-time moms and dads, find this arrangement allays their concerns about the baby's well-being and makes it easier for them to respond to nighttime cries. Once the infant becomes active and alert, however—at about six months old—it is usually a good idea to move her to a separate room.

Not only does such a scheme offer parents time and privacy to return to normal sexual relations, it also helps the baby learn to sleep through the night. When your baby wakes up during the early-morning hours, as babies will, and sees you in the next bed, she may feel encouraged to socialize; waking alone, she is likely to go back to sleep, adjusting to the needs of other family members. Babies do vary, however, in adaptability; if yours seems truly unhappy after a few days on her own, you may want to postpone the change or try having her sleep with a sibling.

A perfect nursery for a newborn is a spruced-up corner of her parents' bedroom. This particular nook is marked as the baby's own by her shelf and christening gown. For her mother and father, having the baby near their bed makes nighttime feedings and comfortings more convenient.

A room of her own

It is also fine to give your newborn a room of her own right from the start, provided it is close enough to yours that you can hear her cry at night. During the day, when you are elsewhere in your home, you might put her down for naps near you, for convenience and peace of mind. The room itself can be small. In fact, tiny infants may feel more secure when they can see a room's walls, since infants are rather nearsighted. Remember, you can always move her to a larger room later on. Such a move is not likely to disturb her sense of security, so long as she has your love and affection as constants in her life.

Buying new furniture

Wherever the nursery will be, there are a few pieces of essential furniture you will probably want to buy or borrow, preferably before the baby's birth. A crib or cradle, a changing table, a bureau or rack to store clothes, and a chair for nursing or bottle-feeding are the usual basics. You can also improvise. You can make a changing table from a dresser or desk, for example, and a single drawer may be enough to hold the baby's clothes.

In general you should choose furniture that you like and that is well made, durable, and affordable. As you examine prospective selections, read the attached tags and test the pieces for ease of operation. Mobility may also be a factor: If you can buy only one cradle or bassinet, for example, you may want a portable one, so that you can move it from room to room. When buying furniture for a small space, look for multipurpose pieces, such as a crib that includes a storage unit. And if you prefer to invest now in items that will last through your child's preschool years, consider convertible furniture—a crib that opens to a youth bed, a changing table that can become a set of shelves.

Unquestionably, you will want any piece you buy to be safe and comfortable for your baby. All surfaces should be smooth, all finishes nontoxic—by law, paint may contain only a minute

Perfectly suited to a baby's needs, this crib-and-dresser combination will later convert to a youth bed. The rails detach, and the three right-hand drawers can be removed and placed on the floor, making room for a new, longer mattress. The stuffed animals along the crib rail give the baby something to gaze at.

amount of lead. Check joints for solid construction, too. Look for sturdy hardware and make sure bolts or screws are properly tightened and secure. A piece should stand foursquare and bear up well when pushed or rocked. See that folding legs on collapsible furniture lock securely in place.

Imagine yourself in the baby's place. He is small, wriggly, and unaware of danger, so look over furniture carefully to be certain there are no gaps where he might catch his head or other parts of his body. Nothing should protrude in any place into which he could reach or roll. Avoid detachable parts that an inquisitive baby might pop into his mouth for examination, and see that fabrics and finishes are intact.

Most of these precautions reflect simple common sense, and high-quality baby furniture is built with them in mind. There are exceptions, however, and older furniture may not meet newer standards, so look closely at all items. Once you make a purchase, follow assembly instructions carefully and heed the manufacturer's advice regarding use and age or weight limits.

Department and furniture stores, children's shops, and dealers in unfinished furniture all supply baby pieces. Ask your salesperson about delivery, service, and replacement of goods damaged in shipping. Order early so your items will arrive in time; many stores will hold furniture until the baby is born.

Secondhand furniture Buying or borrowing secondhand furniture can save you money on articles that you will use for only a short time. In fact, some experienced parents have expressed regret at overspending on furniture and leaving no reserve in the bank for much-needed baby-sitters. So by all means visit secondhand shops and garage sales. Check with friends and relatives, too; many parents gladly loan furniture their children have outgrown.

You will want to go over a hand-me-down piece with special care, since it may have been built before safety standards came into effect. And wear and tear takes a toll on even the best-made pieces. Watch also for paints containing dangerous amounts of lead. Any item painted before 1978, when new government standards were adopted, should be stripped and repainted with high-gloss enamel guaranteed safe for children. Do this a few weeks before the baby arrives, so the fumes will dissipate.

First beds Infants seem to like small, somewhat enclosed beds, such as cradles and bassinets—perhaps for the womblike snugness they offer. Also, these beds usually can be rocked or moved on wheels, providing a soothing motion for an infant. They will be spacious enough for your baby until he is about three months old; then you will need to move him to a crib.

Because a first bed is so quickly outgrown, you may choose not to invest in a full-size cradle or bassinet. One pleasing alternative is a Moses basket, a cozy hooded basket with handles. There are also many safe, portable bassinets—totable ones of canvas, for example. Or, if you prefer, your newborn can sleep in his crib right from the start; use thick bumper pads to bring the sides closer to him.

In selecting a bed for your child, seek comfort and safety. The mattress should fit snugly *(page 45)* and be rather firm, to support the infant's developing bones and muscles. The bed should be deep enough to keep the child from falling out or climbing out; look for maximum height between the mattress support and the top of the rail. Be sure the bottom is sturdy, too; your baby will get heavier. For stability, the base of a cradle or bassinet should be at least as wide as the bed, and any folding legs should lock so the bed will not collapse. If you choose a basket or portable bassinet for your child's first bed, set it on the floor to avoid any risk of its falling or being knocked down.

Cribs   Somewhere between his fourth and sixth month, your baby will become more active, kicking and rolling over, pushing up on his hands and knees. This is the time for a crib, the most important piece of nursery furniture you will acquire. Because the crib will be your child's bed for at least two years, pick one that can withstand a toddler's bouncing and jumping.

Since the late 1970s, cribs have been manufactured according to strict safety regulations. Slats, for example, must be no more than two and three-eighths inches apart; and the height and operation of the drop rail must be designed so that the baby cannot fall out or trip the mechanism. Not all secondhand and portable cribs, however, conform to these standards; should you decide to use one or the other, check the specifications for new cribs at a store and make sure the piece meets them. In addition, do not use a crib with missing slats, and be on the lookout for old paint. If the teething guard on an older crib is cracked or chipped, get in touch with the manufacturer to see about a replacement; when there are decals that the baby might scratch off—and put into his mouth—remove them.

There are certain other crib features you also should inspect. End panels, for instance, should be plain, with no carvings or cutouts where a child might catch his head or his hands. While the current standard allows corner posts to protrude five-eighths of an inch above the rail, many experts recommend no corner posts at all, to eliminate the possibility of an infant's snagging clothing on them and suffocating. Check under the crib, too, for solid steel braces, which help the crib withstand the baby's most vigorous movements. Adjustable metal mattress supports are desirable; they allow you to lower the bed as your baby grows, thus keeping him from climbing out. Check the supports regularly to be sure that all four corner hooks are secured through the slots. Finally, large, swiveling casters will allow you to rock your tiny one gently to sleep, and they also make the crib easier to move from one spot to another. Check to see that they are the kind that have a locking mechanism that will prevent the crib from rolling when the baby is asleep in it.

In terms of appearance, a huge assortment of cribs is available for you to choose from. Cribs come in styles representing various furniture periods, and a few even have canopies. Some are set atop drawers or next to a changing table. And one popular model converts to a youth bed when the child is ready to leave his crib behind.

Mattresses are usually sold separately from cribs. The most important consideration is snug fit: The gap between the mattress and the rails or panels of the crib should be no more than two fingers wide, so the baby cannot get caught in the crack. Note that any used mattress must be disinfected before a baby sleeps on it, and that an innerspring mattress must be examined for any springs poking through the covering. For these reasons, you may prefer to use a brand-new mattress for your child, even on an old crib or bed. In new mattresses, your choice will be between foam and innerspring types. Both kinds provide firmness; foam offers the advantage of light weight and will not provoke allergies. Whichever type of

An antique chest, repainted and given a pad, serves as a changing table. The pad has a safety strap, which must always be used, to keep the baby from falling.

A nursery monitor can free you to step outside the range of your infant's cry. The transmitter is placed near the baby (opposite); the parent wears the receiver (left).

mattress you select, make sure it is covered in waterproof material. You should never try to protect a mattress by wrapping it with plastic bags or sheeting; these things can come loose and suffocate the baby.

Bumper pads, covered in either cloth or vinyl, protect the infant from banging against slats and panels, and make the crib cozy and nestlike. Cloth pads are softer and may last longer; vinyl-coated ones wipe clean. With either kind, it is important that each bumper be securely snapped or tied to the crib in at least six places. Once the ties are knotted, trim the ends to prevent the baby from becoming entangled in them. When the baby can stand, remove the bumpers to keep your little one from using them as a step for climbing out of the crib.

Other baby furniture and equipment

Keep comfort and safety in mind when you select and use changing tables, rockers, and dressers. Arrange your changing table at about waist height, to avoid straining when bending over your infant, and keep her diapers handy under the table. As your baby gains weight, check to see that the table is bearing up under the increased load. And never leave her unattended on the changing table, even when the safety strap is fastened.

A rocker is usually the chair of choice for feeding an infant. It should be sturdy and designed not to tip as you shift about, reaching for one item or another. Armrests will make feedings more comfortable for you, and a table placed nearby is convenient for bottles or burping cloths. Once the baby begins crawling, you will want to watch carefully that she does not catch her fingers under the rockers. Now may be the time to temporarily remove the chair from the room.

You may also want to set aside a special place for your tiny one's wardrobe. In the early months, this spot has only to suit you, but as your child grows, you will want her clothing to be accessible to her. At either stage, a small dresser or armoire or

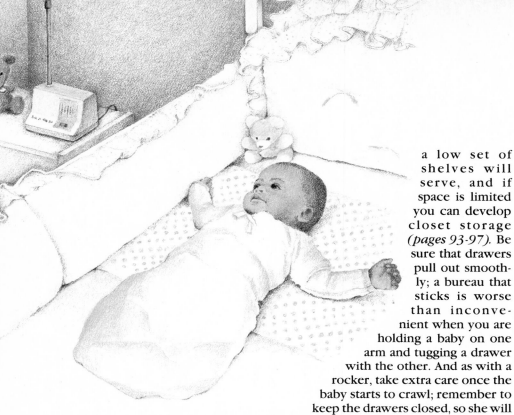

a low set of shelves will serve, and if space is limited you can develop closet storage *(pages 93-97).* Be sure that drawers pull out smoothly; a bureau that sticks is worse than inconvenient when you are holding a baby on one arm and tugging a drawer with the other. And as with a rocker, take extra care once the baby starts to crawl; remember to keep the drawers closed, so she will not be tempted to pull them open and perhaps tip the piece.

In addition to furniture, there are a few other nursery items that will add to your convenience and peace of mind. A hamper for dirty clothes, for example, will help keep the room from becoming messy. A nursery monitor or intercom *(opposite and above)* will enable you to hear your baby when you are in another room. Be sure, however, to pretest the monitor for sensitivity to the kinds of sound your baby makes. Naturally, you will want to avoid growing dependent on the mechanism, but you are bound to feel reassured when you know you can hear your baby's gurgles even as she naps.

Arranging the room   Arranging the baby's room before you give birth will give you a chance to daydream about what it will be like to have a newborn in the house. Try to see the room from the infant's point of view. What would she like to look at in her first months? You might, for instance, put the crib where she can see a beam of sunlight in the afternoon or watch a billowing curtain. For the baby's safety and comfort, be sure the crib or cradle is well away from radiators and drafts, curtains and cords, heavy shelves, and protruding wall lamps. If you want to keep a diaper pail nearby for soaking diapers, buy one with a locking lid to protect your child from the hazard of drowning in it or being poisoned by eating the cake deodorizer. Finally, position the crib so that not even an acrobatic baby can climb from it onto another piece of

For mom F.

I Like My
Lidl Sisdr

Mariel
She loves me
and I love hr
By Marg F.

Making a drawing or a decorated note for the baby's room helps a sibling feel she is an important part of the newcomer's world. Hung near the crib, such colorful artwork as the note above is sure to catch the baby's eye.

furniture. And again, remember to take your convenience into account: You will need a clear path to your tiny one in the dark, for example. The nursery should delight you as well as your child, and your enjoyment of this special room will be mutually gratifying.

No nursery is really complete without the touches that make it special, of course. As well as adding a personal dimension to the room, such items as wall hangings and crib toys will stimulate your little one's senses, piquing his interest in the world around him.

Toys and pictures that have bold patterns with sharply contrasting colors appeal most to infants, who tend to notice contrast more than detail, especially in the early months. Almost all babies respond to bright colors more readily than to pastels, perhaps because these are easier to see against neutral backgrounds. While a newborn baby will be attracted to a very simple design—wide stripes, for example—the same child will prefer gazing at more complicated patterns as he grows older. One study has shown that newborns are drawn to linear motifs, while two- to three-month-old babies prefer circular patterns, such as bull's-eyes.

Keeping these guidelines in mind, you can choose any number of nursery decorations that will intrigue your baby. A modern art poster, for example, may have just the bright hues and simple shapes a newborn likes, while colorful pictures from a garden catalog may interest a slightly older baby. Since motion as well as color attracts infants, crib mobiles are time-honored favorites. Your baby may also enjoy boldly patterned bumper pads or crib sheets, as well as an unbreakable mirror mounted on one of the crib's end panels. A pinwheel spinning in the breeze, a stained-glass ornament shining in the sun, a pair of goldfish flitting in a bowl—all out of reach, of course—are additional bits of whimsy he may find fun.

When decorating your tiny one's nursery, keep his range of vision in mind. Early on, he is quite nearsighted, so place crib decorations and wall hangings no more than a foot away. After a few months, he can focus at a somewhat greater range, and you can move some items farther from his crib. Hang mobiles to one side, since babies gaze sideways more often than straight up. Remember that a mobile is meant for your baby to look at and may not be safe for him to grab and mouth. Keep it out of reach, adjusting its height as the baby is able to reach higher. Change the mobile—and other nursery accessories—now and then, playing to the baby's interest in novelty. And again for safety's sake, when your little one can reach objects and grab them, or can push up on hands and knees—usually about five months—remove any objects hanging over or across the crib; he could get tangled in them.

Finally, be on the lookout for accessories that will appeal to your baby's other senses. You might place a music box near his crib, or a set of wind chimes where they will sound in a breeze. Since touch is extremely important to babies, provide toys that are covered in different fabrics—velvet, satin, cotton—to delight your child. ∴

A three-month-old baby enjoys looking at the hand-drawn paper-plate faces decorating his crib. He is old enough to notice details of eyes, mouth, and nose, but even younger babies are attracted to images of the human face.

The Special Needs of Toddlers and Preschoolers

When furnishing a room for your child, take into account his growth. One morning soon, your once-tiny baby will be standing in his crib, eager to begin the day; and his energy and inquisitiveness may well lead him to try to climb out. This is your cue to start thinking about moving him to a bed. Even if a toddler has not yet scrambled over the rail, when he is thirty-five inches tall the crib loses its basic security since the drop rail, in its highest position, now comes only to his chest. Most likely he will reach this height sometime near his second birthday.

Some toddlers adapt to a regular bed easily, others have difficulty getting used to it. Many children find the new bed uncomfortable or strange; others have a habit of falling out of it. Some may simply be frightened by suddenly having so much open space around them. Thus it is important that you be sensitive to your youngster's capabilities and emotional readiness when deciding to move him out of his crib.

One way to ease a wary child's concerns is to put the bed in his room before removing his crib. Have him nap in the bed or listen to bedtime stories there, but let him return to the crib for overnight sleeping. Soon the crib will seem babyish to him and he will choose the grown-up bed. But a word of caution is in order: Transferring a child from a crib to a bed just when a new baby arrives in the home is not advisable. Make the switch a few months earlier, so your firstborn will not feel he has been displaced from a niche he rightfully felt was his own.

The move from crib to bed heralds a great many other developments. Now your little one can easily get out of bed to travel to the toilet or to investigate a toy. He is increasingly independent and curious, and he needs more space in which to play. As you will see, this puts new demands on his room. It must, of course, be safe and contain furniture he is able to use comfortably. Moreover, there must be space for him to move about easily. And, just as important, as he grows through toddlerhood into his preschool years, his room should increasingly reflect who he is as an individual.

Creating a child-centered room

All the decorating decisions in the nursery, naturally, had to be made by you. But now that your child is a little older, she too can take part in room planning. Her personality is more defined, and because she is beginning to talk, she can express some likes and dislikes. By the time she is a preschooler, she will be better able to give you her opinions—and will have a good deal more of them. She will like being consulted about curtains and carpet, shelves and tables. And she probably has some definite ideas of her own, preferring frills to crisp lines, for example.

Of course, whether your child is a toddler or preschooler, you have the right to veto a suggestion you deem unsafe, inconvenient, or too costly. But be open-minded. Having your small one help plan her room builds her confidence in her own taste and ability to make choices and adds to her sense of herself as an interesting and significant person.

Choosing a bed   Your toddler's first bed can be anything from a mattress on the floor to a conventional twin-size bed with box springs and a frame, as long as the mattress is firm enough to support growing bones and muscles. Even if you pick an older bed for your youngster, you may want to buy a new mattress, to ensure her comfort. You will also want to fit the bed with guardrails, to keep her from falling out; most children need these until about the age of three. And tucking the sheets in tight also helps lessen the danger. For a few months after you remove the railings, you might lay cushions on the floor beside the bed, just in case.

As for size, a youth bed suits a toddler perfectly but will be outgrown in just a few years. It thus becomes a rather expensive choice. Unless your youngster's crib converts to a youth bed or you can borrow one, you are better off buying a good-quality, twin-size bed. A toddler will soon grow into it and it will last him through childhood.

You need not limit your choices to conventional box-spring beds, however. A low platform bed is one possibility. A captain's bed is another. A trundle bed is still another; it rolls out from under the main bed, providing room for overnight guests or for

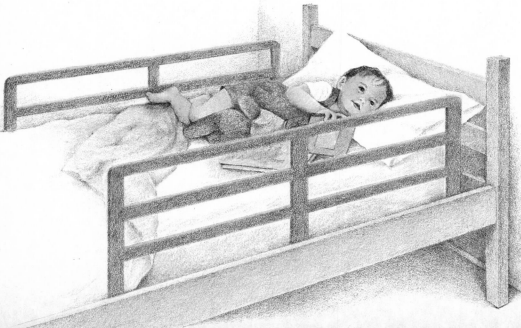

Safety rails on both sides of a toddler's first bed help him feel secure by keeping him from tumbling out or getting caught between the bed and wall. For a bed that lacks them, safety rails can be bought separately at juvenile-furniture stores and added on.

yourself when your child is ill. Bunk beds have terrific appeal for almost any child, whether or not he shares a room with a sibling. Even an only child has plenty of use for bunk beds; he is bound to like the cavelike feel of the bottom bunk, the top-of-the-mountain feel of the upper one, and the fact that a friend can sleep over. Stacked bunks are best used when the child is old enough to sleep in them without falling out, although you can invest in a set now and leave the two side by side until you feel your young one is ready for the experience. Examine bunk beds carefully before making a purchase, with a particular eye to the many safety considerations involved *(opposite).*

Other furniture Now that your child is mobile, the other furniture in her room becomes more important. In deciding which pieces from her babyhood to keep and which to weed out—and what other items to add—take into account her size and abilities. The more she can use the items in her room on her own, the more independent she can be.

If, for example, you have been keeping her clothes in a large, heavy wardrobe, now is the time to adjust the shelves or rods to her height, or change to something smaller and more manageable. Arrange her toys on low shelves, so that she can get at them herself. And you will want to take another look around the room, to make sure there is nothing in it that could now harm

Snug in the trundle bed where she regularly sleeps, a two-year-old enjoys having her visiting older cousin nearby. Next year, when the toddler moves up to the higher bed, she may still sleep with the trundle pulled out, as a step up and a soft spot to land should she fall. Daytimes, the trundle bed is pushed in, freeing floor space.

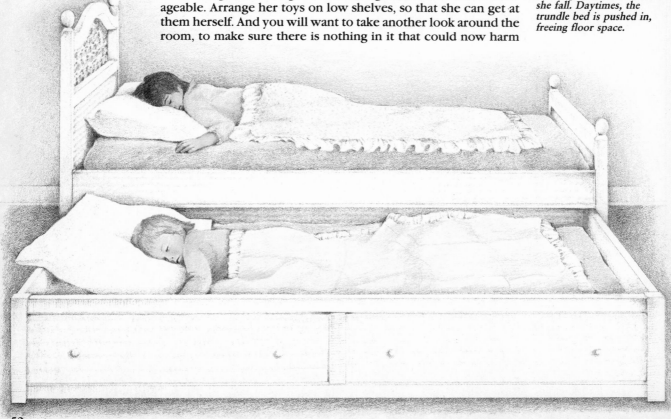

Bunk Bed Safety

Eager though your child may be to have double-decker beds in her room, it is best to buy the kind that can be used as two low beds first and wait until sometime near her sixth birthday before stacking them. The timing should depend not on her exact age, but on her maturity and motor skills; be sure she is sufficiently well coordinated to avoid falling from the top bunk or becoming entangled in the ladder.

In shopping for bunk beds, look for the safety features illustrated below. And once the beds are stacked, take precautions to ensure your child's continued safety. To begin, make clear to the child that the beds are for sleeping and quiet play only, because she could injure herself if she fell from the top bunk. Teach her that she must use the ladder attached to the bedframe, rather than climbing to the top bunk on chairs or other furniture. To enable her to see when descending at night, leave a night-light on, or install a wall lamp where she can switch it on easily. Examine the beds every few months to see whether frame, slats, and rails are firmly in place.

While guardrails on the lower berth may be removed when the child is old enough, those on the upper berth should be left on around all four sides. There should be no more than three and a half inches between the rail and frame, to prevent the child from slipping under the rail and falling from the bed. Railings should rise at least five inches above the mattress.

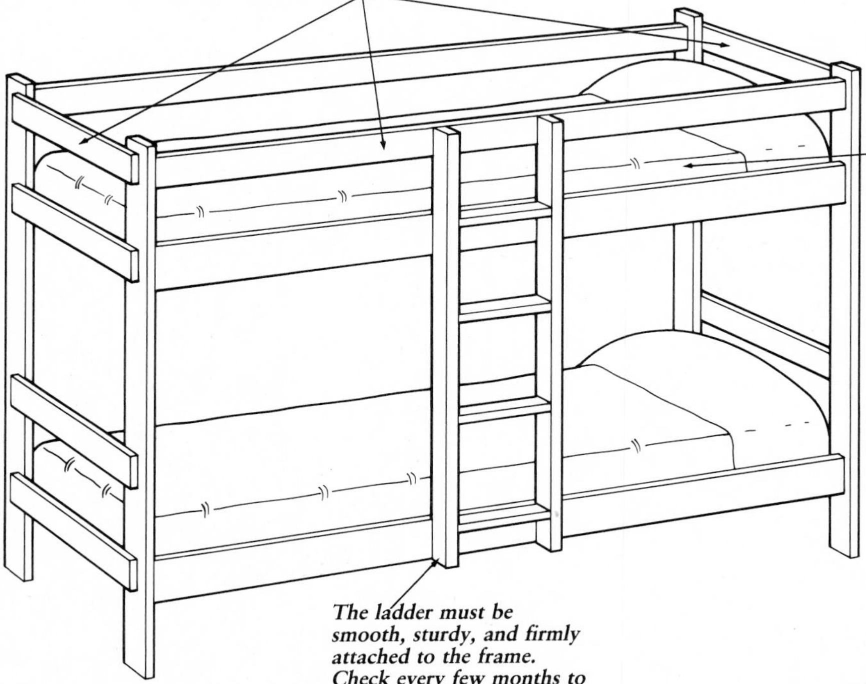

To avoid one common bunk-bed hazard, be sure the mattress size—standard or long—matches the frame size. A standard mattress in a long frame leaves a five-inch gap between mattress and footboard, a space where a child can easily get stuck.

The ladder must be smooth, sturdy, and firmly attached to the frame. Check every few months to see that the joints are secure; a child can be as hard on the ladder as on playground equipment.

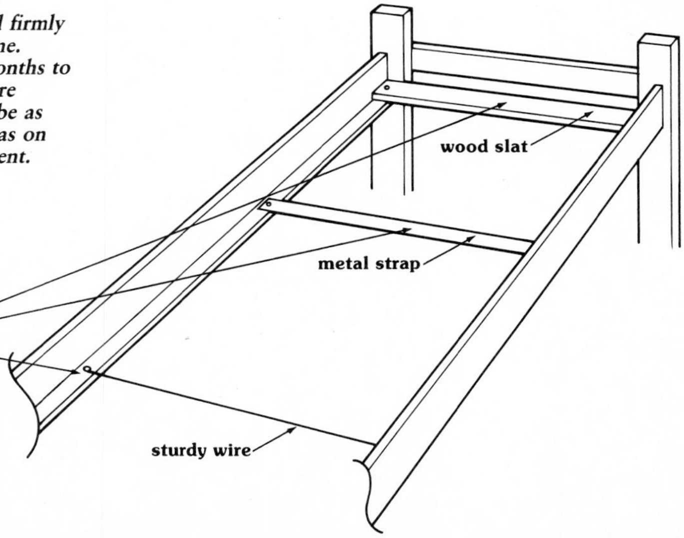

Make sure both the bedframes have crosstie mattress supports to hold the mattresses firmly in place. Wood slats, metal straps, or sturdy wire can all do the job.

wood slat

metal strap

sturdy wire

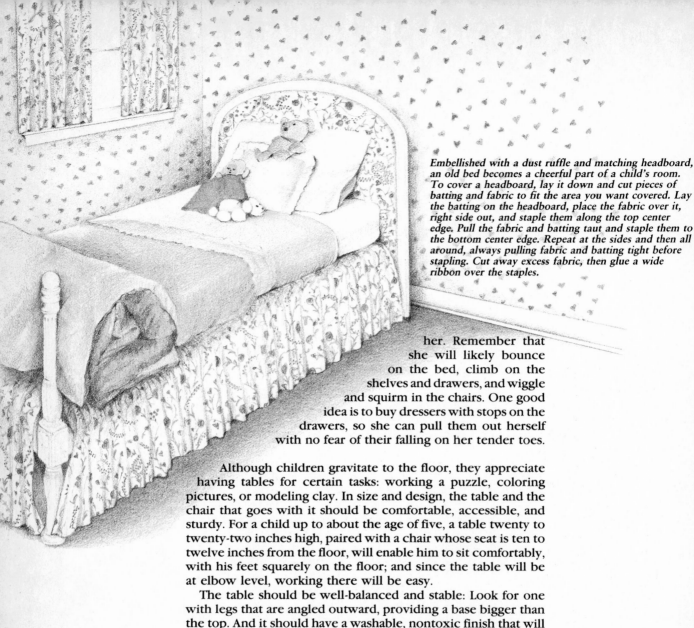

Embellished with a dust ruffle and matching headboard, an old bed becomes a cheerful part of a child's room. To cover a headboard, lay it down and cut pieces of batting and fabric to fit the area you want covered. Lay the batting on the headboard, place the fabric over it, right side out, and staple them along the top center edge. Pull the fabric and batting taut and staple them to the bottom center edge. Repeat at the sides and then all around, always pulling fabric and batting tight before stapling. Cut away excess fabric, then glue a wide ribbon over the staples.

her. Remember that she will likely bounce on the bed, climb on the shelves and drawers, and wiggle and squirm in the chairs. One good idea is to buy dressers with stops on the drawers, so she can pull them out herself with no fear of their falling on her tender toes.

Although children gravitate to the floor, they appreciate having tables for certain tasks: working a puzzle, coloring pictures, or modeling clay. In size and design, the table and the chair that goes with it should be comfortable, accessible, and sturdy. For a child up to about the age of five, a table twenty to twenty-two inches high, paired with a chair whose seat is ten to twelve inches from the floor, will enable him to sit comfortably, with his feet squarely on the floor; and since the table will be at elbow level, working there will be easy.

The table should be well-balanced and stable: Look for one with legs that are angled outward, providing a base bigger than the top. And it should have a washable, nontoxic finish that will not chip or splinter. A wood table with a laminated plastic top is a good choice. Molded plastic tables are also excellent and have the added advantage of being light enough for the youngster to move on his own. You might even consider using an extra-heavy cardboard box as a temporary table. Cover the edges with tape for increased stability, then cut a kneehole in one side and draw up a low stool or a big cushion as a seat.

Your child's bedroom furniture should also include a few chairs. With the table, pair a sturdy, straight-backed chair, one preferably without arms so that your child has room to make broad, sweeping strokes with his crayons and paintbrushes. The chair legs, like those on the table, should be slightly angled. If you use folding chairs, make sure there are no places where fingers can be caught or pinched. Your child would probably enjoy having a small rocker in his room; its motion can make him feel comforted and because the motion is under his control, powerful. Avoid any chair that is top-heavy, and if your child rocks too wildly for your peace of mind, affix corks to the bottoms of the rockers to limit their sweep. Finally, you might also want to provide your youngster with at least one soft seat: a beanbag chair, for example, or a large, soft cushion.

Since the furniture for your child's room may consist of new, unfinished pieces, hand-me-downs, or donations from friends, you will no doubt want to spruce it up. You can easily do so with a natural oil finish, stain, or paint. For an even more personal touch, you may wish to put your imagination to work and decorate appropriate pieces with wallpaper, fabric, or stenciled or hand-drawn designs *(page 56)*.

Since unfinished furniture has been sanded at the factory, about the only preparation you must give it before applying your finish is to sand it just enough to remove any dirt, scratches, or stray wood fibers. If you are restoring an older piece, additional steps are required before refinishing. Begin by checking the piece against current safety requirements. Then make sure the furniture is in good shape, repairing any broken parts and filling in dents or holes with wood filler. Strip off the previous finish if necessary, then sand the wood until it is smooth.

Not only, of course, do toddlers grow, but so does the number of their possessions; it is not unusual for a three-year-old's playthings to fill shelves, drawers, and baskets, and still spill over. The floor becomes an ever more important part of the room; your youngster is likely to use it for playing, thumbing through his books, and talking with you. And once he begins to play with friends, the need for floor space becomes even greater.

A drop-leaf tabletop secured to the wall provides a sturdy surface for doing artwork. The table folds down when not in use, and will be remounted higher up as the child grows taller.

55

Custom Decorating a Child-Size Bench

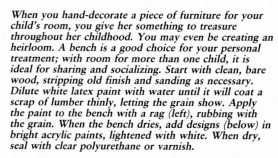

When you hand-decorate a piece of furniture for your child's room, you give her something to treasure throughout her childhood. You may even be creating an heirloom. A bench is a good choice for your personal treatment; with room for more than one child, it is ideal for sharing and socializing. Start with clean, bare wood, stripping old finish and sanding as necessary. Dilute white latex paint with water until it will coat a scrap of lumber thinly, letting the grain show. Apply the paint to the bench with a rag (left), rubbing with the grain. When the bench dries, add designs (below) in bright acrylic paints, lightened with white. When dry, seal with clear polyurethane or varnish.

Motifs Children Love

It is a good idea, therefore, to try to keep a central area in the youngster's room clear. Situate the furniture against the walls, and make toy storage easily accessible to your child so that clutter does not prevail.

Room decorations

Accessories enliven and individualize a room, whether it belongs to a five-year-old or a thirty-five-year-old. Unusual pillows, patterned sheets, colorful wall hangings, and treasured collections on display will make your youngster's room enjoyable and truly her own. Form a partnership with your child in choosing the accessories for her room. You can guide her and she can guide you, and the partnership will lead to results that please both of you.

When it comes to decorating a room around a single theme, it is best to use a light touch. Theme rooms, while fun, can be limiting, unless you have the means to change them as often as a child's interests and tastes change. It is far easier, for example, to replace an animal-print bedspread than to repaper an entire room done up as a jungle. And an overly defined theme can curb a child's imagination, channeling her thoughts in only one direction.

Wall décor

Finding things to put on the walls is certainly no problem. Travel posters, maps, flags, kites, quilts, fabric panels, and animal placemats all qualify. Using letters and words as well as pictures will help familiarize your child with the alphabet and stimulate his interest in reading.

Wire-hung pictures can be dangerous if a child decides to lift them. Instead, secure the pictures with mirror clips, available in hardware stores; or for lightweight items, use adhesive pads. Try draping a fishnet on one wall and clipping postcards and photographs to it. Or get a magnetic bulletin board and let your child rearrange the items on display as he likes.

Other embellishments

The sky is the limit when it comes to eye-catchers. Objects that hang from the ceiling are

Mounted on foam board at a framing shop, an appropriate sheet of gift-wrap adds zip to a child's room. Posters and collages can be similarly mounted.

fascinating to children—a piñata, say, or a kite with its tail stretched across the room. A bird feeder placed just outside the window will add a living dimension. Even words and numbers that she has drawn in crayon with your help can be hung up for decoration. A cuckoo clock makes her giggle and brings numbers and time-telling into her world in an amusing way. Indeed, letters, words, and numbers begin to mean something to her now, and having them in her room will encourage learning.

For a truly personal touch, help your little one make a throw pillow for her bed. Have her draw a simple shape on a large piece of paper—a cat face, for example. Cut out the resulting pattern, pin it to two layers of fabric, and then cut out the pillow itself. Sew the pieces partially together and stuff the pillow with bits of foam. After sewing it shut, stitch on details with yarn.

Doubtless you and your small one will discover other ways to make her room pleasant and appealing. You cannot go far wrong if you listen to her wishes and observe her behavior. Together, you will come up with a room that reflects both your taste and hers and that is adaptable enough to change as she does—a room where she will find contentment and inspiration. ❖

An alphabet border crayoned by a child working closely with his mother is a bright addition to a preschooler's room. Together they picked objects to illustrate the letters. Besides its decorative appeal, the alphabet serves an ongoing educational function.

A Shared Experience

Sharing a room can be a positive experience for small children. If all goes well, the give and take of daily life will help the youngsters learn to cooperate and be flexible. Moreover, the intimacy of the experience can deepen their feelings for each other and help build enduring ties.

Rooming together also may enhance the positive emotions and behavior that siblings learn from each other. An older child, for instance, who comforts her younger sister in the dark, is showing her ability to empathize. She is likely to feel proud of her courage and grown-up status and thus gain in self-esteem. At the same time, the smaller child feels protected, safer, and braver, simply by being with her older sibling. Interestingly, most children who share a room are less fearful than those obliged to sleep in a room alone.

Deciding to have children share

In some homes, siblings must double up because space is limited. Perhaps it is time for an infant to move from the parents' bedroom, or perhaps a room must be freed for a baby-sitter or a parent's home office. But even when necessity does not dictate sharing a room, children may prefer it. A toddler, for example, who admires his older brother may especially like having him close by at night.

In making up your mind about whether your children should occupy the same bedroom, you need to take several things into account. One of them is the children's ages. While siblings of widely different ages can share a room, ideally no more than three or four years should separate the youngsters; otherwise, it may be too hard for them to communicate and to accommodate to each other's habits and schedules. If there is already a great deal of rivalry between two youngsters, no matter how close they are in age, you will want to try to resolve the tension before having them room together. Another consideration is the children's gender. Usually a boy and girl can room together comfortably until about the age of seven or eight, but you should take your cue on this from the youngsters themselves. If either child expresses discomfort earlier, be attentive.

It is wise to consider your own motivations for moving children into the same room. If a shortage of space is the reason, then of course you must proceed, looking for the best possible arrangement. You may even want to think about giving the master bedroom to the children who are going to share, and taking a smaller room for yourselves, since young children need plenty of floor space for their many activities. But before you undertake any move, you should ask yourself whether your decision springs more out of a need of your own rather than out of a true need on the part of your children. Perhaps you were an only child who wished for a sibling with whom you could share a room, or perhaps you had an especially good relationship with a brother or sister and would like to see it replicated through your offspring. Make sure that the setup you propose really suits your children, no matter how much you may think they will benefit from the experience.

Planning for the change

Assuming the family has agreed that two siblings will share a room, proper timing and planning will ease the adjustment to the new arrangement. The transition will go more smoothly if your little ones have similar bed-times, or at the very least, if the baby is now sleeping soundly through the night. You might want to keep a portable crib on hand, so you can wheel a fussy sibling into another room while the other child sleeps.

In the case of older children, you will naturally want to discuss the upcoming change with them at least some weeks in advance. Often, a younger child is all enthusiasm, while an older sister or brother is unhappy about giving up valued privacy and prerogatives. Assure your elder youngster that you will respect her needs as much as you can. Try to provide at least one spot where she can go to be alone, to play, or just to sit and dream. This might be a nook in the living room, or perhaps a part of the dining room. Consider as well making creative use of the house rules and privileges in helping your children adjust to new rooming arrangements. If the new plan calls on the older child to give up some space, she will feel the loss, but you can make sure she also gains. Providing she is old enough, you might want to push her bedtime back just a little, as an extra sign of her elder-sister status. And give her a say when arranging the room that she is going to share, taking special care to help her store her things so that her new roommate cannot get into them. Wall-mounted shelves just out of the younger child's reach will head off many a tearful scene—and in addition, your older child may find them the best toy-storage system she has ever had.

Arranging the room

How you arrange the children's shared room will depend on the personalities of your children and on how they feel about each other at the time of the move. Young children who already have

an open, easy relationship may enjoy sharing the room as a whole. In this arrangement, each youngster will have her own bed and dresser, and at least one shelf for personal collections and toys. Floor space and furniture such as table and chairs can be shared. This often works well, especially while the children are preschoolers. As the youngsters get older—or if they have strong feelings about privacy—you may want to make a clearer division. The sections need not be identical or even perfectly equal; it is more important that they reflect each child's interests, tastes, and personality.

Even if you and your young ones choose not to apportion space in the room, you should promote individuality in a number of more subtle ways. The bed and the area around it, for example, usually become a child's personal territory. You might

With their bunk beds in an L-shaped arrangement, twin girls can spend time together when they feel sociable, or they can be in separate spaces when they prefer to be alone. This plan also creates space for a chest of drawers under the upper berth.

have the youngsters each choose their own sheets and spreads, or even select different kinds of beds. Drawers and shelves can be color coded, and area rugs can be used to define territories. You can paint walls different colors or have each youngster design one corner of the bedroom.

To give your children a sense of separateness, consider arranging beds so that the youngsters are not always facing each other. You might, for example, put the beds at right angles, with just one corner touching, then fit a small table into the space at their junction. Bunk beds, sleeping lofts, and platform beds give children a chance to enjoy separate time, too, as each sibling can gaze out at a different level of the room.

A special bonus of the bunk-bed arrangement shown on the previous page is a niche behind the chest, a secret play area the children enter easily from the bottom bunk.

Should you want to clearly define separate areas within the room, there are many ways to do it. The idea is to create a partition of some sort; it may be low or high, it may reach across the whole room or across only part of it. Furniture—bookcases, dressers, wardrobes, even storage cubes—can serve as one kind of partition. Place the pieces in the center of the room, either back to back or next to each other, with each piece facing a different direction. Each child has his bed on the side of the room that his dresser or cupboard faces; and if the back of his sibling's bookshelf or dresser faces his side, he can use it as a bulletin board. Bunk beds can be used to create a partition. Place them in the center of the room and arrange one child's furniture on either side of the beds. Then, to increase the sense of two individual areas, attach a sheet of plywood as a screen running the whole length of one side of the lower berth; mount another along the upper berth, but on the other side. Thus, each youngster looks out onto his own side of the bedroom.

Aside from furniture, you can

When Siblings Live Together

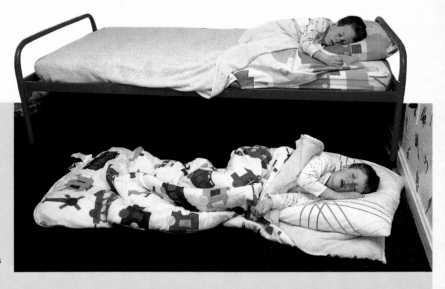

66 I got Bill and Joey's rooms set up soon after we moved, to make our new house feel homey for them. But after about a week, one would always wind up in the other's room, asleep on the floor by the bed. So now the little one sleeps in a sleeping bag on the floor by his brother's bed. On weekends, they decide whose room to sleep in and call it a sleepover. So they have these two wonderful rooms and every night there's one that's empty. 99

66 Everyone told me my girls need their own space—they're three years apart and have very different interests. So I gave them their own rooms. But you can skip those words of wisdom because the girls really just want to be together, and so they're sharing again. Sometimes I hear the two of them giggling until ten o'clock, and they go to bed at eight-thirty! 99

66 I thought it was really important that Kevin and Colleen each have a separate space. For them, just having a bunk bed was enough—that way, Kevin could climb up and get away to a place where his little sister couldn't go. 99

66 Claire, our two-year-old, has shared a room since her younger sister was born. At first we worried about how they would deal with it when one cried, but they block it out, and neither of them has ever kept the other awake. 99

66 Our five-year-old son needs his shelves high enough to protect his things from his little brother. And the little one needs the floor. The five-year-old knows he can't leave his toys where the baby can get them. And so he picks up his things and puts them away—and am I ever glad. 99

66 Tyler and Christopher did get into 'yours' and 'mine' a lot more when they were in separate rooms—if one borrowed something from the other's room, the other would be looking for it and not find it. Now that they're in the same room, sharing is a little easier because things are in sight. 99

66 Even though we have an extra room, both our girls share. One day the younger one decided to move out. She spent most of the day shifting her things to the other room. But then she realized she'd have to sleep alone, and so she spent much of the next day moving her things back in. 99

66 Our five-year-old daughter sleeps upstairs and her two older sisters share a room downstairs. Lately she's been saying, 'I'm lonely. I want to share a room with Jane.' She's very independent, but I think sometimes she feels left out and a little bit jealous. 99

66 My five-year-old and two-year-old boys have shared a room since the two-year-old was a baby. At first, the sleep schedules were a problem, but we all lived through it. We had no choice. When the baby used to cry and cry and cry, I would take Greg, the older one, out of the room and let him sleep either in our room or on the couch. And when Greg would go into his own room to sleep, we would always say, 'Hush, don't wake your brother. Be very quiet and don't say a word.' And we always had storytime out in the hallway, since the baby went to bed first and we didn't want to wake him. 99

66 Kenny and Michael had their own separate rooms, but Michael, the youngest, was always too afraid to sleep in his room alone, so he would run down the hall to Kenny's room and get into bed with his brother. So, we decided to put him out of his misery and let them share the same room. We had bunk beds, thinking that would allow more space. But in the middle of the night, we'd hear Michael yelling, 'Kenny, come down here and get into bed with me 'cause I'm scared!' So then we put them on the same level—both beds on the floor—to see if that would help, and it seemed to help a little bit. 99

66 I think that even if we ever live in a house with enough bedrooms to accommodate everybody, our two youngest daughters will always share a room. I believe that it will be really important for them to maintain that special bond. The two girls will probably always be friends in a way our first two children never will be. 99

A Snug Retreat for Three

A few basic design techniques and a little creativity can transform even a small bedroom into one that several children happily share. With furniture around the perimeter—some of it scaled to the size of the occupants—and light hues enhancing the sense of space, the ordinary nine-by-eleven-foot room depicted on these pages comfortably holds three sisters. As the three-dimensional view (*below*) shows, the arrangement manages to accommodate their beds and storage units and still gives them enough of a floor area to play on.

Fitted all around with guardrails, the loft bed against the left wall gives the oldest girl, six, both a sleeping area and her own private daydreaming space. Tucked under the bed, a desk painted white offers handy working and storage space. Next to the desk is a minicrib where the youngest child, six months, sleeps. Beside the loft, a standing closet uses corner space, and in front of one window, the top of a white chest of drawers doubles as a changing table. Another chest of drawers sits along the opposite wall. On the near right wall, a full-size crib with drawers underneath and at one end provides sleeping space for the middle girl, two.

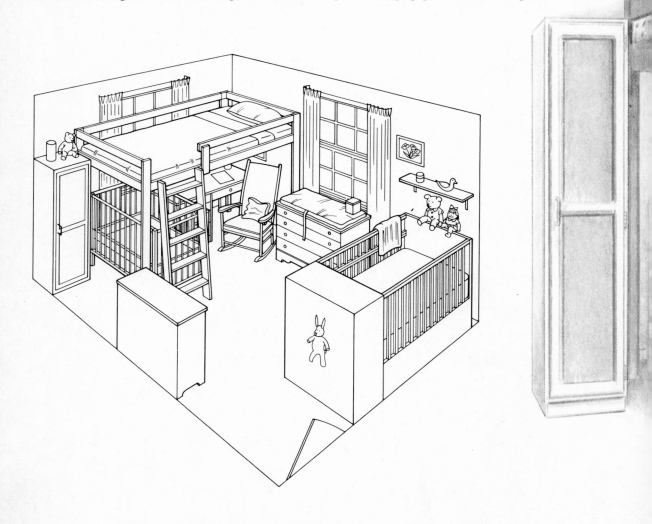

As the closeup partial view of the room (above) illustrates, the loft arrangement opens up floor space considerably and helps parents organize to meet their new baby's needs. Because the bunk stands six feet high, they can get at the minicrib easily; the rocker sits near the crib for feeding and rocking the infant.

also use screens, curtains, or office-style partitions. Folding screens, for example, divide the room but give it a light, airy ambiance. Office partitions create a more solid barrier, a kind of wall on which the youngsters can hang pictures and memorabilia. For stability, you will probably want to attach one end of any screen to a wall. And curtains hung from a ceiling rod give a fresh feel to the room. Many of these dividers can be folded or pushed back to make one large space. So can a sliding or folding wall, installed in a ceiling track. At night, you can extend the wall to divide the space for sleeping; then, during shared playtime, slide it back.

Making a permanent division
If the children are older or feel strongly about having separate rooms, you may want to consider erecting a plasterboard wall. Keep in mind that you need a relatively large room for this to work effectively and that the arrangement works best when each child has a window. (If there are no windows, consider putting one in the new wall.) Every wall of each section should be longer than the floor-to-ceiling height, or the spaces will seem cell-like. In a smaller room, consider building a low wall, rising perhaps only halfway to the ceiling. Or you can extend the wall only partway across the room, leaving some joint floor space.

Whichever method you choose, you may need the help of a carpenter in putting up the wall: It should be sturdy and well anchored. Having a professional room designer look over the room before any work is done may be worth the expense, too, especially if you want to erect a full-length, floor-to-ceiling wall. The designer can help ensure that each child will get enough light, air, and heat, and can suggest ways to create an extra closet if one is needed.

Learning to share
However you divide the room, give the children some time to adjust to the new situation. Be sensitive to any problems they may have. When possible, hear out the arguments; try to offer solutions that take into account both youngsters and that evenly distribute the burden of adapting. There are, for example, a number of ways to resolve territorial disputes, short of drawing a chalk line down the center of the room. Avoid setting up win-or-lose situations, in which one child gets her way one time, the other the next; try instead to find a point of agreement or compromise. And at times, you will find that you simply have to lay down the law.

You might tell a younger sibling, for example, that although she is able to reach her sister's favorite doll, she is not allowed to play with it; explain to her that everyone is entitled to her own things. Or you may need to insist that an older youngster get into bed more quietly, so that she does not disturb her sister's sleep. And be sure to praise her behavior when she does. Sometimes a small action can work wonders. If one of your children is feeling her individuality has been swallowed up by the move, for instance, give that youngster the opportunity to choose something special for her side of the room—a throw rug, perhaps, or a funny poster.

Finally, be ready for the new arrangement to have some impact on you as well as on the children. For one thing, it may be harder for you and the children to keep the room tidy. And at least at first, your small ones may be inclined to stay awake later, talking and giggling. All things considered, though, most children will enjoy sharing a room for at least a few years in early childhood. And they may even take their cues from their mother and father, who, after all, have also had to learn to share a room with each other. ❖

Brothers Divided

Parents of two young boys have used furniture partitions to grant a measure of privacy to each of the growing siblings. As shown in the three-dimensional drawing *(right)*, the boys' beds have been placed end to end along the back wall; bookcases and inexpensive plastic shelves divide the room where the beds meet. Each brother thus has his own corner and his own desk for art activities and, later, schoolwork. They use the remaining area for games and active play; their shared space also contains a small set of drawers for odds and ends, a dresser, and two closets *(shaded areas)*.

Making Storage Space for a Growing Family

Keeping your home neat and orderly after the arrival of the new baby is not the impossible task it may sometimes seem. Instead of throwing up your hands in surrender, now is the time to think creatively about where and how to increase your storage space. One way is to rearrange existing space, another is to find new space in places you may never have considered before. On the following pages are a host of ideas to help you get started.

Remember that neatness, per se, is an adult, not a child, priority, and that some "mess" may be beneficial in a preschooler's life. At this stage of your little one's development, she needs to explore the world around her; what you see as clutter may be an unavoidable part of that exploration. Nonetheless, children appreciate order, too. They like finding things in familiar places all the time, and they like knowing where things go. Most experts believe that small children need an ordered environment to thrive.

Unlike an adult bedroom, many children's bedrooms are multipurpose rooms. Besides providing a place to sleep, they may serve, at various times of the day, as a playroom, a room for entertaining guests, an art studio, even a place to eat. And because so many of a preschooler's activities take place on the floor, floor space is almost always at a premium. By providing your child with the right kind of storage facilities to meet all of these varied needs, you encourage her to take care of her own belongings. At first, her motivation in helping you pick up may be to gain your approval, or perhaps to identify with you through imitation. But as she grows older, she will find, like the little girl enjoying a "talking" story in her streamlined room at right, that neatness and order make life more enjoyable, more controllable, and easier—to say nothing of enhancing the feelings of self-esteem and self-respect that she derives from her newfound independence.

Assessing Storage Needs

The old adage A place for everything and everything in its place can sometimes seem like an unattainable goal to a tired parent confronted with a child's cluttered room. But with a little effort, that happy state is not quite so difficult to achieve as it might seem. The key to success is organization, and the best place for you to begin is by making an inventory of your youngster's belongings; they will probably fall into six general categories—toys, games, clothing, artwork, books, and such equipment as carriages and strollers.

Deciding what to eliminate As your first step, sit down—preferably with your child close by so that he can have input—and go over the items in each category, weeding out those that are no longer useful. Get rid of clothes that are beyond repair, too small, or no longer worn. Save the best for hand-me-downs, or if you like, give them away. Some families keep separate boxes in the garage for discards and move them along when they are filled.

You will also want to take out of circulation any books your child has outgrown and any toys and games that no longer

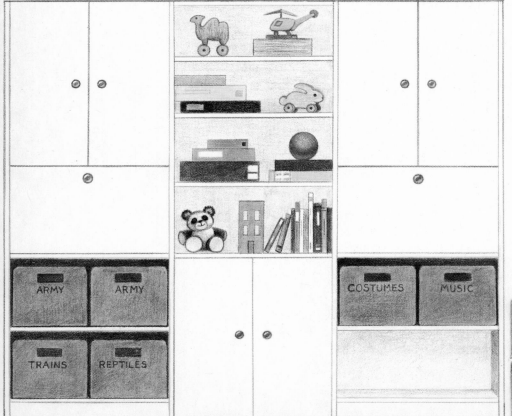

This wall-storage system combines parent-accessible storage on its upper levels and space for toys in labeled bins below. Each bin is small enough for a preschooler to pull out and carry around. Additional bins, filled with old toys, are kept in the attic (opposite). To rotate toys, simply exchange a bedroom box for an attic box.

interest him, are broken, or have parts missing. Possessions that your child is particularly attached to but rarely uses should be stored where he can see them or get at them. A decorative wall shelf, perhaps positioned above windows or a door, will take a number of these; but as the accumulation grows, you may want to consider setting up a keepsake box. If you have an attic or basement, store the box there, label it with his name, and note its contents on top—perhaps with some descriptive drawings—so that he as well as you will know what the box contains. Tell your youngster where the box is and allow him to go to it as often as he likes. Now and then, he may ask to reinstate a particular toy or book to his active collection, but more typically, things that are out of sight will soon be out of mind as well. At that time, those possessions can join the other pass-alongs in the garage.

Preserving what you keep

As your next step, cull out things that your youngster no longer uses but that may have sentimental or future value, such as gift clothing from grandparents, out-of-season gear that can be worn next year, and the various mementos, large and small, that you or your child want to preserve.

Prepare clothes for storage as you would adult wear, taking time to mend and clean them first. Fold synthetics and cottons, pack them in cartons, and seal the boxes shut. Stuff shoes, boots, and hats with tissue to maintain their shape and box them too. Hand-wash and block woolen goods, and place them along with mothproofing chemicals in protective garment bags or a cedar chest, if you have one. A silk christening gown can be gently washed and pressed at home; but if it is trimmed with lace or other embroidery, or has a lining or similarly complicating details, you will probably be better off turning the job over to a professional dry cleaner.

Delicate toys and artwork also deserve special care. Wrap the most-precious items in acid-free tissue paper rather than newsprint, which yellows and cracks over time. Use sturdier paper for less fragile keepsakes, and put them in cardboard cartons. Do not forget to remove any batteries that might corrode or leak. You may want to frame the best of your child's paintings and drawings for permanence. The rest of the youngster's artwork should be stored in metal, rather than cardboard, boxes; the metal provides better protection against moisture, heat, and poor ventilation.

Again, list the contents on the boxes so that you will be able to identify them without having to unpack everything. It is also a good idea to number the boxes and key them to an inventory, so that you can see at a glance what they contain. In recording hand-me-down clothing, note size or the age you expect your child will be when he is big enough to wear it. That way you can avoid the frustration of rediscovering, one year too late, that the "almost new" snowsuit you put away for your youngster is several sizes too small.

Limitations on everyday items

Everything that is left over has won the right to remain in your child's room. But you may still find yourself confronted by a daunting miscellany, especially if your youngster is one of those children who likes to save everything, including all the rocks, bottle caps, seashells, corks, marbles, and old tennis balls that he has managed to pick up.

Rather than discourage this normal trait, you may wish to keep your little one's possessions under control by making only a portion of them accessible to him at any one time. The other items can be put into storage and rotated back to his room, perhaps once a month or so, at which time you can put away some of the other things.

Keep a seven-day supply of clothes in a visible storage area where your youngster can get at them readily. In this way, you help limit the number of items he has actually to manipulate, making it easier for you and him to keep order. At the same time, you provide him with enough variety to allow for choices when dressing. You might also place a hamper in a convenient spot and encourage him to drop his daily discards into it.

Maintaining the system

Once you have a system in place, try to gain your child's co-operation in maintaining it. Try to make sorting through her possessions and letting go of some of them an ongoing process. Encourage her to help you with this chore. Let your youngster watch as other members of the family go through their own weeding-out procedures, so that she recognizes this process as a routine part of life. •ː•

Instilling a Sense of Order

Children are not born with a sense of organization. They acquire it gradually. You can help by setting up a regular schedule of meals, playtimes, naps, outings, and bedtime for your baby, and by keeping his room relatively neat while allowing for variety *(Expert's Box, page 74)*. When he is between eighteen and twenty-four months old, he may be ready to be introduced to the notion of picking up after himself. If you motivate him well and provide him with the proper storage facilities, you will probably find that he will begin to cooperate.

Organizing your child's room
A child cannot cope any better than an adult in a room overloaded with possessions. Make it your task to set up a storage scheme that reflects your youngster's various needs. If possible, involve him in planning the arrangements for his room. Have him stand and raise one arm to show you the limits of his reach. Let that height define the area for storing items he routinely uses—everyday clothes, favorite toys and games, books, stuffed animals and dolls, perhaps a tape recorder or a phonograph, modeling clay, paints, and the like. Talk to him about ways to display his treasures, perhaps a rock collection or an assortment of tiny plastic animals. Given such special treatment, they are bound to seem even more special and precious to your little one, and out of pride the child will want to be careful playing with them and putting them away. And be attuned to your child's logic.

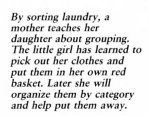

By sorting laundry, a mother teaches her daughter about grouping. The little girl has learned to pick out her clothes and put them in her own red basket. Later she will organize them by category and help put them away.

An Expert's View

Why Orderliness Counts

Opinions differ about the importance of nurturing a sense of order in a growing child and providing her with a structured environment. Some parents believe that both are critical to later development; others think they are unnecessary, and when overdone may even trigger an adolescent rebellion against neatness. Still others say that tidy habits and order are important, but not for infants. I believe that because environment is actually a child's first teacher, order—not neatness—is essential to her overall development, especially between the ages of six and twenty-four months, when she is maturing at a very rapid rate.

Order in a home does not mean that everything is neat and clean. Rather, it means that belongings are kept in a manageable fashion and that the lives of the people who live there proceed in a logical progression. Young children in particular are sensitive to the regular scheduling of events—mealtimes, bedtimes, playtimes, naptimes, storytimes, and the

like. Early on, they begin to learn by taking in everything they see and hear, and sorting it all out. In an orderly home, they quickly learn to differentiate between objects, discover how to group them, and come to realize that day-to-day living is composed of a predictable series of balanced steps and procedures. If the environment in which a child begins this learning is overcrowded and haphazard, such learning will be hindered; she will not be able to feel the rhythm of the day and will not learn that there are predictable places and times for certain activities. It is important to have variety in a little child's world, to stimulate her mind and her muscles with new toys, new sounds, new faces, new substances, and new activities. But unless this variety occurs within ordered boundaries, the child may be overwhelmed and become inhibited and passive rather than active in her explorations of her world.

In a number of tests designed specifically to assess the development levels—both motivational and intellectual—of infants, experts have measured just how

much of a determining factor the early environment can be. Time and time again, children coming from homes considered more orderly scored higher than those from disorderly homes. And even by the time they reach school age and have learned to control and manipulate their surroundings more and more, environment continues to play a major role. In preschool settings, children who work and play in more ordered environments exhibit more focused social behavior and more active involvement in tasks, which may result in more logical thinking patterns. Then, their ability to do schoolwork well and to solve problems may be enhanced.

But if you still think that it cannot make any difference to an infant how clutter is piled in her room, I can only urge you to think again. The people and things in a little person's world are the only tools she has for learning, and every one of them has an impact.

Theodore D. Wachs
Professor of Psychological Sciences
Purdue University, West Lafayette, Ind.

You might think it sensible, for example, to put pencils and crayons in one place and paper in another; but he may perceive them as belonging together because that is the way he uses them. Thus, he might prefer a single container for all his drawing materials. If he likes to play in a particular corner of his room, do not then crowd it with furniture or storage units. You may even want to rethink using a traditional bureau for his clothes. Some children prefer open storage to closed drawers because they can see their possessions and feel a greater sense of control over them. For large toys, cubbies at floor level work well. In a child's imagination the cubby for his dump truck can become a garage, the one for the stuffed bear a cave, and so on. Smaller possessions, clothing included, also benefit from having their own individual spaces, or if this is not feasible, their own area within a larger divided container.

Learning to appreciate order

When your child has storage facilities that meet his needs, he can begin to experience the satisfaction that comes from having things under control. Encourage him to play a greater role in organizing his own possessions by giving him tasks that are within his range of ability, such as putting away his toys at the end of play, or stowing his muddy boots in the garage when he comes in from a morning of fun outside.

Help him to see cleanup as an indivisible part of play rather than a separate, unrelated chore. Before he abandons one activity and begins another, you might suggest "When you clean up all your blocks, you'll have room to play with your puzzles," or "Here are some toys that we need to put away so they don't get lost or broken." And then praise his follow-through. Soon your youngster will begin to see that being orderly can serve his own self-interest.

The concept of grouping

As your child grows accustomed to picking up after himself, introduce more-sophisticated notions of organization, such as grouping objects by similarity of use or shape. Here, a traditional oversize toy chest may work against your purpose, for playthings consigned to it inevitably find their way to the bottom and almost every effort at uncovering a particular one ends with

After a play session with his dad, a little boy cheerfully puts his toys away while pretending to be a construction worker cleaning up after a job. By lending his son his hard hat and some gloves, the father has made cleaning up a game in itself.

others being tossed onto the floor. Show your child instead how to put groups of related objects together—stuffed animals in their own big box, mittens in the mitten basket, books in the bookcase, and so on.

Take advantage of everyday opportunities, such as sorting laundry or shelving groceries, to demonstrate that keeping order is an important factor in making life run smoothly. You might elicit your youngster's assistance with other household chores by asking "Can you find all of Daddy's clean socks and put them in a pile?" or "Can you find your pajama top and bottom and put them together?" When he reaches for something that falls outside the category, chat with him about what makes that item different from the others. Play a little game of delivering the piles to the right places and have him help you put them in their proper drawers.

Fitting the chore to the child

By the age of three, your child may be comfortable enough with the concept of grouping that she can carry out a succession of explicit instructions. But she is still a long way from knowing what "Please go clean up your room" means. You need to be more specific in describing the particular task you want her to perform. Some parents list chores on a chart, with each one identified in pictures and labeled—"dirty clothes," "books," "bed," and so on—to remind their youngster what is expected of her. When the child completes a chore, her accomplishment is acknowledged by a few positive words of reinforcement and a star on the chart.

But whatever method you use, try not to overpraise your little one or focus too much on the reward. You will want your youngster to appreciate the value of being neat, and not become conditioned to the idea that by putting her belongings away she will always be rewarded.

It is also a good idea to choose a specific time of day when the room is to be tidied up and then to keep your child company while she works. Four-year-olds can do reasonably well picking up if they receive consistent supervision, but most children this age are still too little to perform many everyday chores by themselves. But resist the urge to do the job for her. Instead, try breaking tasks down into steps that are within her capabilities. Then lead her through them. Your preschooler may not be able to tuck in sheets and blankets, for example, but she can smooth out the bedspread or quilt. And do not be too fussy about the results. By letting her do as much as she can, you are fostering her pride in her own accomplishments. ❖

Fresh Approaches

No matter how logical, practical, and child-friendly the storage system you set up, it can still fall short of inspiring your youngster to learn to start picking up after himself. One good way to get him in the habit is to provide him with amusing opportunities for assembling things in their proper place, such as the clothesline scheme for hanging stuffed animals pictured below.

On the following pages you will find several other whimsical ideas for helping your youngster assume greater responsibility for his possessions. You can convert a bookcase, for example, into diorama-like shelves with painted backdrops that will yield fun but invite order as the logic of storing the toys with the related scenes becomes apparent to him. You may wish to use old soda crates, drawer organizers, wall grids, and typesetter's trays to house his seashells, rocks, and other tiny collectibles. Your child is bound to enjoy moving the items from one space to another, and the empty slots in his storage containers will serve as reminders that some of his treasures are missing and must be found. He might also like having movable storage units to play with—boxes on casters that will allow him to transport his toys anywhere in your household, then pack them up when he is through with them, and deliver them back where they belong.

Organizing Stuffed Animals

*Clothesline strung across a wall at a child's height
makes a handy organizer for stuffed animals. With
easily removed sturdy clothespins, the child can take the
toys down, pin them up again, or rearrange them. As
the collection grows, simply add another length of line.*

Adapting Carrying Cases

Old traveling cases make good carryalls for toys, and with some paint and imagination, they can be turned into integral parts of play. The doll's wardrobe above is closeted in an overnight case; its exterior has been painted to look like a house, its inner lid, a bedroom wall. The briefcase at right has been decorated with a castle scene for an army of toy knights.

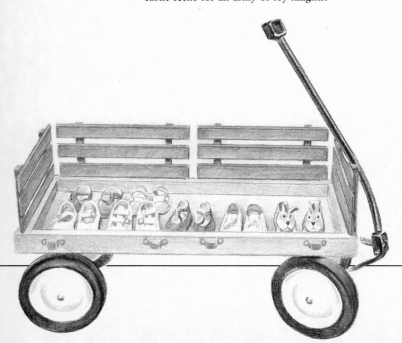

Rolling Storage That Tours the House

With a small wagon like this, a child can make a game of gathering up errant belongings, here footwear. When not in active use, the wagon stands in a corner of the bedroom, its cargo ordered and accessible. A doll's carriage or a toy wheelbarrow can also be used as an entertaining mode of storage-to-go.

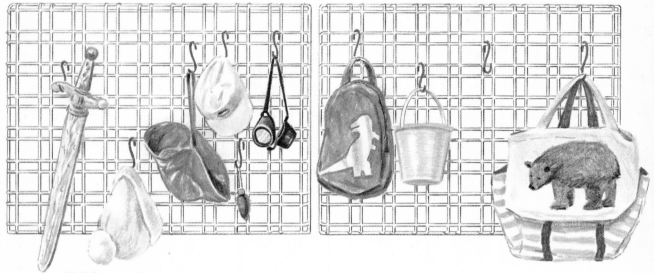

Wall Storage Units

A wall grid like the one above allows a child to store various possessions and express her decorative flair simply by moving the S-hooks from rung to rung. Grids are sold in the housewares section of most department stores. The typesetter's tray below functions similarly; its cubbies encourage a child to play at rearranging the miniatures that they hold.

Turning a Bookcase into a Stage

A two-shelf bookcase serves as both an attractive storage area and an amusing place to play. On the top tier, the boy's mother painted a roadway for his collection of miniature cars and trucks. Inside the case on the next level, she created a castle courtyard as the setting for his array of medieval warriors. The bottom shelf is fitted with a removable piece of artboard, painted by the child himself to provide a mountain landscape for his dinosaurs. At right are substitute scenes created by the youngster for other imaginative play: a farmyard for a collection of animals, an ocean view for boats and ships, and a household interior.

Improvised Storage

There is no need to spend large sums of money setting up a multipurpose storage system for your child's belongings. The basic components may exist right in your own home in the form of everyday items—cartons, boxes, coffee cans, plastic tubs, or jars. Generally, the more unusual and inventive the container, the more your child will like it and the more fun he will have using it. Take a look around the house and see what kind of things you can find.

Before recycling an old container, you should clean it thoroughly, washing it with soap whenever feasible, and cover any sharp edges with tape. If the container is made of wood, smooth the surface with sandpaper to prevent splinters. You may also want to spruce it up by applying a fresh coat of varnish or lead-free paint.

Avoid altogether any container that once held toxic materials. In addition, you should be very cautious about using chests or footlockers with heavy lids that could crash down suddenly and injure your child or that could lock accidentally, trapping him inside. If the unit happens to be equipped with a hinge, it is important to add a spring-loaded lid support that will hold the lid open. The usual adjustable-friction lid support is not reliable enough for small children. As an extra precaution, you may want to drill breathing holes in the piece to guard against the possibility of suffocation.

Matching the container to the object

Try to find containers that correspond to the size of the objects you plan on storing. Toy soldiers, doll clothes, crayons, table-tennis balls, baseball cards, marbles, and jacks call for small solutions. Such common household receptacles as shoeboxes and shoe bags, thread caddies, oatmeal boxes, kitchen cannisters, metal bandage boxes, ice-cube and silverware trays, plastic food-storage boxes, breadbaskets, and even mailboxes are perfect for this purpose. Metal coffee cans with smooth, dull rims and snap-on plastic lids or wire salad baskets also work well for holding small items.

For larger toys and possessions, try using old fruit and vegetable crates from the supermarket; small trash cans; wastebaskets; and partitioned wine racks and boxes. An extended family of teddy bears or a collection of costumes can be kept under control in a brightly patterned cotton laundry bag. Unwieldy items like plastic baseball bats, a sleeping bag, or a tent can be stored in such oversize containers as wicker hampers. Also consider stashing large things in the fiberboard drums that wallpaper rolls come in.

Stored in several plastic jars originally used for baking materials, easy-to-see crayons, marbles, and an assortment of blocks provide the room's young inhabitant with several clear-cut play choices.

Check out neighborhood housewares, office-supply, sporting-goods, Army-Navy, and hardware stores to search for other storage possibilities. You may come across items you might never have dreamed of buying for their original purpose but now can see as being useful to you. Plastic laundry baskets, dishpans, and pails can be mobilized for storage. A clear plastic tray, partitioned into compartments to hold nuts and bolts, can serve as an organizer for your child's smallest toys.

Stackable plastic boxes, which are patterned after milk crates, are made specifically for storage purposes and come in a variety of models and colors. You might equip your baby's nursery with a couple of them to store diapers, receiving blankets, or crib sheets. You are bound to find new uses for them as your little one gets older. Depending on how you turn their open side, the cubes can be used as bookshelves, record cabinets, stools, and tiny tables.

Why labeling is important, too

A one-word explanation of contents—"Shoes," "Cars," "Puzzles," and perhaps a picture of same, either painted or traced on the storage unit—will promote a sense of order. The exposure to printed words in connection with items your child cares about may well whet his interest in learning to read. As he gains mastery of words, the labels become that much more helpful in guiding him to the things he is looking for. The labels can also have an aesthetic value of their own when they are carefully executed, bringing a visual consistency to otherwise disparate containers. ⋯

Finding and Increasing Storage Capacity

Almost never, it seems, does a house or an apartment start out with enough storage space, particularly of the convenient sort. When a household includes one or more children, the situation can become even worse. Often the rooms most deficient in storage space are the children's bedrooms, which in nearly every home tend to be small. Add to this the fact that children are particularly adept at accumulating hard-to-put-away items, and many families find themselves facing a storage crisis.

On the following pages are some suggestions that can help you solve your storage needs and, at the same time, add comfort and order to your home. Doubtless, you will welcome the ideas that pertain specifically to a child's room. But because children tend to stake out every corner of the house for play, particularly rooms in which their parents and other family members spend time, you will probably also need to find ways to utilize and convert spaces and equipment throughout your entire home. When you put your mind to it, you may find areas besides the traditional basement, attic, and garage that you can develop—perhaps in the kitchen, the living room, the hall, and the bath. In addition, you should take into consideration space that you may never have thought of using for storage, such as walls, ceilings, and the backs of doors. By no means exhaustive, the ideas offered here are intended to inspire you to look creatively and constructively at your entire home and find workable solutions of your own.

Keep in mind that what works well for storage at one stage in a child's development may not be appropriate at another. When your youngster is a baby, she has no need to reach her belongings. You are free to choose storage arrangements that suit your own convenience. But somewhere near her eighteenth month, your little one will begin to develop a sense of her own identity and her own territory and will want to keep her possessions in places that she feels belong to her. And it is important, developmentally, that she have them.

An empty bookcase provides open storage for a girl's clothes. Everything is accessible, although she will have to get up on tiptoe for a few months to reach the top shelves.

Start your planning by making a survey of the built-in and free-standing cabinets that might be available for storage. Some of them may be underutilized because they are no longer needed for the purpose for which they were originally designed. With a little rearranging, perhaps one or more of them could become a satellite toy center.

This notion of spreading toy storage areas around the house has merit on several counts. By dispersing your child's possessions, rather than trying to localize everything in a single space, you take some of the storage pressure off his room and provide him with a fresh change of toys as he roams about the house. And by allowing your youngster to have a designated space in rooms other than his own, you are enhancing his sense of belonging to the family.

Crawlers and toddlers love to be where they can watch their mothers, and since many mothers spend a substantial amount of time in the kitchen, a floor-level kitchen cabinet can be one of the better places to put toys.

Other places to investigate are the den, the family room, and the downstairs hallway. You might find a spot for coloring books and crayons. A low desk drawer, a cubby in the base of the stereo cabinet, or the bottom shelf of a bookcase might be a handy location for board games and puzzles. A hall linen closet, its lowest shelf removed, can become a tricycle garage. And do not forget other household crannies, such as the area under a staircase. Perhaps a row of child-high hooks for coats and hats could be installed there, or some stacking boxes for snow boots and rain gear. There may also be room for a few bulky items—snowsuits, skis, hobby horses, games, and train sets. Some families install rolling storage bins under the stairs. When the bins are in place, they can look built-in, but their casters permit them to be moved out into the play area.

When checking your cabinets, closets, bookshelves, and bureau drawers for possible space, also evaluate their present use to see whether you can make some practical changes. For example, guest towels might as easily—and more attractively—be rolled up and stored in a wicker basket on the bathroom floor as kept hidden away in the linen closet. Likewise, extra bedsheets and blankets, neatly stored in a basket or on a quilt stand, can supply a spot of color to a bedroom corner, while the chest that held them is given another storage function. And in the kitchen, pots and pans might be hung on the wall or from a rack, lending the room a cozy, country look while freeing up valuable near-the-floor cabinet space.

Using bathroom spaces

To many children, the bathroom seems made for play, a place to have fun with boats, floating toys, rubber ducks, and sopping, squeezable sponges. When not in use, every one of these items needs to be stored somewhere, and often the edge of the tub will not do. You can buy a variety of inexpensive shower caddies and other devices made specifically for bathrooms that will do double duty as toy holders. Another solution is to net the items in a nylon string bag and hang it from one of the tub fixtures. For larger collections, a plastic milk crate that sits near the tub offers a neat, waterproof solution. Another possibility is a tiered rack with vinyl-covered wire baskets; it can be stood in the corner, along a wall, or on top of the toilet tank, with toys kept in the bottom baskets, and clean towels, washcloths, and other items in the top ones. Such a rack is available in bathroom-supply and housewares stores. If your sink is not built into a vanity unit, you can create additional storage space by attaching a floor-length apron around the bottom edge with several lengths of plastic gripping cloth. There you can neatly and conveniently keep everything from toys to extra toilet paper.

Unconventional storage sites

Belongings that you and your child use infrequently, such as seasonal clothing and seasonal toys, can be put away in places that you may never have considered using for storage. Such

This child never has to call for her bath toys when she wants them because they are stored right in the tub, in a bag suspended from the faucet. When she finishes playing, the rebagged toys drip dry.

hideaways can be found in, under, and behind standard furniture. You might, for example, spread an attractive floor-length coverlet over a corner table in the living room and use the space beneath for a collection of sailboats, beachballs, buckets, and shovels. Or, you might stash board games, a folding easel, a painter's drop cloth, and a box of watercolors under the sofa if it has a dust ruffle that will conceal them from view. And by positioning the back of the sofa a few inches from the wall, you can tuck a fold-up stroller or a sled in behind.

Many older homes come equipped with built-in window seats. Besides providing a wonderful site for reading and relaxing, these delightful architectural features customarily come with a wealth of storage space concealed beneath a cushioned bench. But such seats can pose a safety threat if not adequately equipped. As with the toy chest and footlockers mentioned earlier *(page 82)*, window seats should have spring-loaded safety supports or other styles of safety hinges installed. And the storage section of the seat should have air holes or openings drilled into it to provide ventilation, should your child climb inside and accidentally become entrapped.

Even chairs have storage capabilities. If an armchair is positioned away from foot traffic in a corner of the room, the unused space behind it can become a parking lot for a toy wagon. And a standard wooden chair can be turned into a child's private reading center, with the space framed by the front legs, side rails, and center brace serving as a miniature bookcase.

Ideas for the bedroom

Bedrooms have hidden storage potential, too, but usually it is the bed itself, with its expanse of horizontal space between box spring and floor, that offers the most room. The easiest way to put this wasted space to use is to store boxes and the like underneath, hiding them with a dust ruffle and a bedspread. If you place the items to be stored on a large piece of sturdy cardboard, you can use it to pull them all out at once when you want to get at them. For long-term convenience, an under-the-bed drawer that glides in and out on wheels might be worth the extra cost. Because the drawer has a handle, even your pre-schooler will be able to pull it out and push it back in. Since ready-made rolling drawers are common items in home-furnishings stores, you can probably find something to fit your requirements. Some drawers come with a plastic dust-protector that can be fitted over stored items.

Try a little ingenuity. You may discover that a box with partitioned compartments designed to hold adult shoes, for

Dolls and stuffed animals that are not in use can be attractively stored on a high shelf. This out-of-reach but still visible area is also perfect for collectibles, such as porcelain dolls or model airplanes.

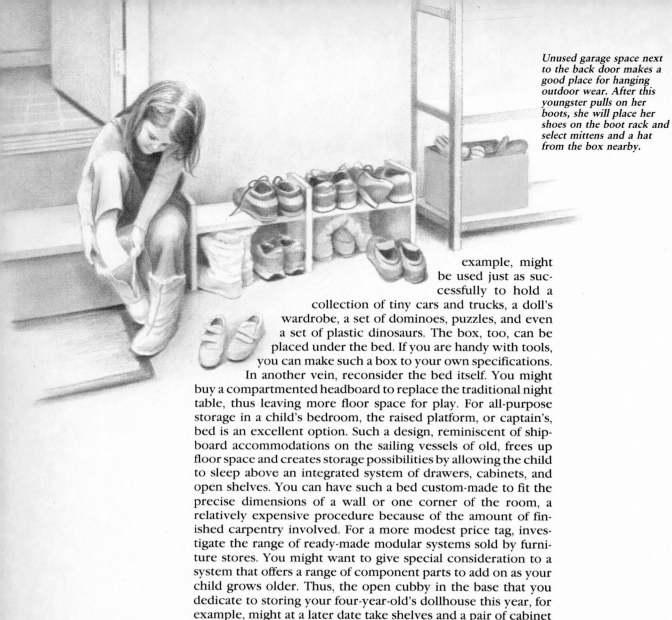

Unused garage space next to the back door makes a good place for hanging outdoor wear. After this youngster pulls on her boots, she will place her shoes on the boot rack and select mittens and a hat from the box nearby.

example, might be used just as successfully to hold a collection of tiny cars and trucks, a doll's wardrobe, a set of dominoes, puzzles, and even a set of plastic dinosaurs. The box, too, can be placed under the bed. If you are handy with tools, you can make such a box to your own specifications.

In another vein, reconsider the bed itself. You might buy a compartmented headboard to replace the traditional night table, thus leaving more floor space for play. For all-purpose storage in a child's bedroom, the raised platform, or captain's, bed is an excellent option. Such a design, reminiscent of shipboard accommodations on the sailing vessels of old, frees up floor space and creates storage possibilities by allowing the child to sleep above an integrated system of drawers, cabinets, and open shelves. You can have such a bed custom-made to fit the precise dimensions of a wall or one corner of the room, a relatively expensive procedure because of the amount of finished carpentry involved. For a more modest price tag, investigate the range of ready-made modular systems sold by furniture stores. You might want to give special consideration to a system that offers a range of component parts to add on as your child grows older. Thus, the open cubby in the base that you dedicate to storing your four-year-old's dollhouse this year, for example, might at a later date take shelves and a pair of cabinet doors and be used for keeping blouses and sweaters.

Walls and doors The walls and doors of your youngster's bedroom or playroom offer other good opportunities for keeping all kinds of possessions out of the way. In many instances, the very items you are storing can double as decorative elements, adding flair and style to the room. A review of the possibilities might begin with any of several relatively simple strategies for hanging things up. A handsomely framed corkboard or a magnetic bulletin board can accommodate notes, a calendar, cartoons, posters, snapshots, and a changing exhibition of personal artwork. A pegboard, bolted firmly to the wall and equipped with hooks, can help organize a disparate collection of tools, mittens, and magic tricks. Secure the hooks with tape to keep them from popping out of their holes when something is grabbed, and position them at levels where your child will not readily bang into them. If you like, trace the outlines of each item on the pegboard so that your youngster will know just where to return it.

Plastic-coated or heavy-duty paper bags with handles, decorated with bright colors and lively designs, can also be used to create a wall storage unit. You can use just one or a whole collection, hanging them on the wall with hooks or by some other creative means. Depending upon their sturdiness, you can use the bags to hold all kinds of light objects, including dolls' clothes, socks, shoelaces, hair supplies and accessories, plastic jewelry, and art supplies.

A coatrack consisting of a horizontal row of wooden or plastic pegs or metal hooks with padded tips set in a length of decorative ironwork or wood can be affixed to the wall at child's height as a place to park funny hats, decorative duffel bags filled with dolls' clothes, or dress-up clothes. A pegged chair rail placed at a convenient height will permit child-size chairs not in use to be hung out of the way, thus providing more room for play. A drop-front table anchored to a wall can be flipped up to serve as a surface for board games, coloring, and finger-painting. When the space is no longer needed, you have only to collapse it by releasing the supporting safety hinge that is on the underside.

The tracks of a train set can be accommodated in similar fashion. Permanently attach the tracks to a rigid sheet of painted plywood or fiberboard. So that there will be room for the tracks when the unit is in place against the wall, first nail or screw a strip of wood about one inch thick to the baseboard and then attach the board, with the tracks in place, to it with strap hinges. The board can be kept upright against the wall with a hook. You can easily lower it when your child wants to play with his trains. Paint the surface facing the room the same

Coatracks installed at two levels in a back-door entranceway meet the needs of both adults and children.

color as the wall or decorate it with a railroad motif. You may need to add a brace or a collapsible leg to it so that when the board is in the down position it will be properly supported. Store the trains separately in a wall-hung basket nearby.

For a collection of cuddly creatures, or an assortment of beachballs, soccer balls, and footballs, you might suspend a see-through hammock from wall to wall across one corner of the room and fill it with the toys. Tuck dolls' dishes and dollhouse furniture in a cluster of ceiling-hung wicker baskets, the lot attached to a cord and pulley so that your little girl can bring them down when she wants to play with them.

And put all sorts of blunt hooks on the back of your youngster's bedroom door—one for pajamas, another for a robe, another for a favorite reading pillow to which you have sewn a large hang-up loop. The back of the door is also a fine place to tack a shoe bag, only let this shoe bag be attractively adorned with colored yarns or patchwork and let each shoe pocket be filled with a toy or doll.

After you have exhausted the possibilities in your child's room, turn your attention to the rest of the house to see if some of these same principles and ideas can be applied to the walls and doors in other rooms. Not only will you be creating new storage space, you will also possibly be adding new decorative elements to your home.

Shelving   Hanging shelves can provide additional storage room. You might consider installing a narrow shelf one foot or so below the ceiling in your child's room. On this shelf you can display an extended family of your youngster's stuffed animals, rag dolls, or other attractive toys in a lively and interesting way. All you need are some standard shelf brackets, wall anchors, and wooden boards. You may wish to paint the shelf in an accent color, making it a dramatic feature.

In a spacious room, you can put up a variety of shelves at various heights to hold different objects. Presuming that you want your child to have access to at least some of these on a regular basis, and that there is floor space to spare, you might include a set of library ladders. Some rolling library ladders run on metal tracks mounted on the upper part of the wall or shelving and are best installed by professionals. More practical for most children's rooms is the stepladder version; for safety's sake, you should choose a unit that is well weighted for stability and equipped with handrails. Your youngster will soon discover that the stairs have other uses as well: They are great props for

A three-year-old selects a pair of socks from a basket on the back of his door, hung there by his parents to make it easy for him to learn how to choose his own clothes. The bottom basket contains T-shirts and underwear.

amateur dramatics and fine perches for teddy bears and other favorite playmates.

And finally, for all-around storage that is attractive as well as useful, there is nothing to beat the integrated systems that cover an entire wall. Based on a three-dimensional modular grid, these units typically include open and closed cubbies, pegboards, hanging racks, and perhaps a bulletin board, all in one visually and structurally unified design.

If a permanent system is applicable to your situation, and you are equipped to carry out such a project, you may want to build the basic structure from scratch, using pine boards or plywood and the appropriate hardware. Such a system is generally attached to wall joists and possibly to floor and ceiling frames as well, so that it becomes a more or less permanent part of the room. Keep it flexible to allow for the child's changing needs and tastes by providing adjustable support for shelves and drawers.

Alternatively, you might want to investigate some of the modular wall systems that are available at home-supply and furniture stores. Most of them can be assembled in a variety of ways in order to meet different storage needs. In many of these systems little or no anchorage is required to walls, floor, or ceiling; instead freestanding uprights adjust to your required height and are held in place by spring-loaded ends that press against floor and ceiling without marring them. Movable pins, clips, and other sorts of hangers are used to hold the horizontal parts of the storage system together.

One type of wall storage that is well suited for children's rooms combines vinyl- or paint-coated steel supports and shelving with hanging wire-mesh shelves and drawers. Mounted in freestanding frames, these storage systems leave virtually all the stored material visible so that your youngster can easily find whatever he wants. Or you could try a system that includes doors and drawers as an alternative to open storage if you prefer.

Check with specialty closet stores, housewares, and department stores for choices. You might also want to investigate places that sell industrial shelving and office supplies. Your child may love having his very own filing cabinet—just like Mom's or Dad's. Another unique addition to your youngster's room could be a stand-up locker, very much like those that are found in a school or gym. If you buy a standard metal one you can decorate it yourself. There are also plastic models available that come in a variety of bright colors and sizes. Sometimes the most unlikely items seem to make the best storage units, especially if your youngster has a hand in picking them out and putting them to effective use.

Garages and attics   Garages and attics are natural locations for storing children's gear. Here too, the more things you can keep off the floor and out of the way, the better. Unused bicycles and tricycles, for example, can be hung overhead on specially designed supporting hooks that screw firmly into the walls, beams, or rafters. Balls, bats, life jackets, and sand pails can be bagged and hung high along the walls. Or if there is space above open rafters, you can create a storage loft by laying sheets of interior plywood across the members and then nailing them in place. Be sure to keep an inventory and floor plan of what you put up in the loft, and display it nearby for easy reference when the time comes to retrieve items.

You can help your older preschooler learn to be responsible for delivering his sled or tricycle to the right location by marking rectangles on the floor with heavy tape or paint to designate the proper slot for each possession. Remember, though, that however appropriate garages and attics may be for storage, they are usually not good play areas for young children. Lawn and carpentry tools, insecticides, rock salt, and many other potentially dangerous objects and materials may also be kept there. Moreover, the walls and floors of attics and garages tend to be rough and unfinished, which can lead to injuries during youngsters' uninhibited play sessions.

Make sure that the garage or attic space your child will use for his possessions is separated from the less-safe storage sections. Explain to him which areas are off-limits and why. Accompany him on his first ventures into the attic or garage so that he becomes familiar with the places where his toys are kept. Using caution from the outset will help both of you feel more confident about his safety. ❖

Closet Space That Suits a Child

Closets have the potential for being the most versatile of storage solutions, combining hanging space for coats, jackets, dresses, and pants with stacking and shelving space for toys, games, and other items. But not all children's rooms come with closets, and those that do are likely to have closets designed with an adult in mind. So, one way or another, you are probably going to have to do some improvising to provide the kind of storage your youngster can use conveniently and self-confidently.

If you are starting from scratch and want to create storage space in a room that has no closet, your first thought may be to construct one. But this can be expensive, both in terms of dollars and floor space. A simpler solution is to provide a freestanding storage rack, such as the one below, that can be set up in the room itself. A hall stand of wrought iron or wicker, a child-size wooden valet, a wall shelf with provisions for hangers, or a clothes tree *(page 94)* are other attractive ways to accommo-

date coats, jackets, and other gear. A freestanding wardrobe, or armoire *(page 95)*, is a more elegant substitute for closet space; it offers the commodiousness of a closet with the lasting value of good furniture.

In a room with a conventional closet *(pages 96-97)*, consider first how it can be adjusted to suit your child. Take into account his size and the kinds of items he will need to keep there. Establish an easy access section for everyday wear, a less accessible section for clothes that he wears occasionally, and a third area for stuff he rarely uses but still wants nearby. Then, you can equip the closet accordingly, using tension rods and movable shelves that can be manipulated as he grows. If you have the carpentry skills, you might try your hand at putting up your own rods and shelving. Otherwise, there are a wide variety of prefabricated closet-adapter systems that you can purchase at hardware or home-center stores and install yourself.

Designed with a child's stature in mind, this freestanding storage unit features accessible hanging space on one side with stacking shelves and a shoe rack on the other. Such units come in various sizes and configurations. Some are equipped with drawers.

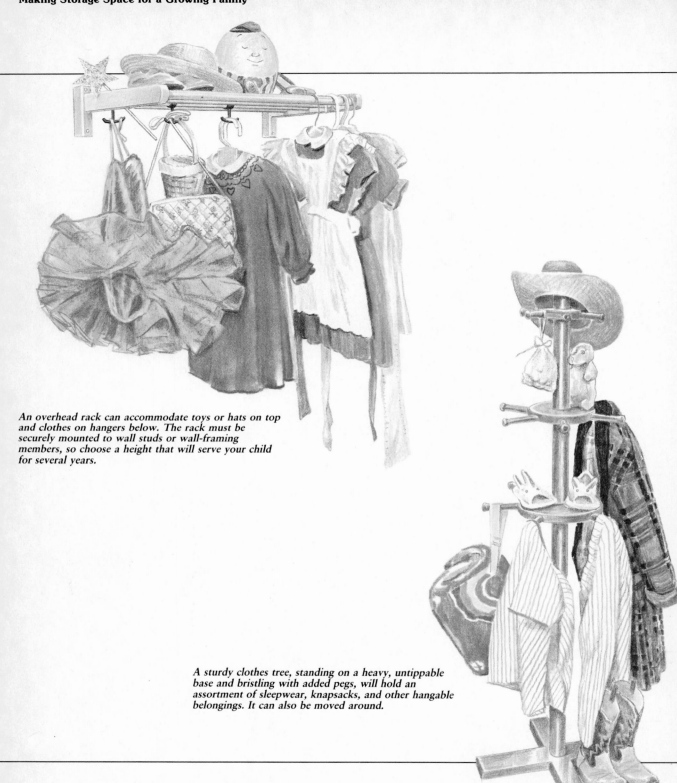

An overhead rack can accommodate toys or hats on top and clothes on hangers below. The rack must be securely mounted to wall studs or wall-framing members, so choose a height that will serve your child for several years.

A sturdy clothes tree, standing on a heavy, untippable base and bristling with added pegs, will hold an assortment of sleepwear, knapsacks, and other hangable belongings. It can also be moved around.

An old-fashioned armoire, equipped with adjustable tension rods, provides nearly as much space as a small closet. An elegant alternative to open storage, a well-made armoire represents a considerable investment. Yet, a good one can become an heirloom that its owner will use and cherish when a grownup.

This wide closet has been modified to make room for a growing child by the addition of two space-expanding accessories: a set of wire drawers on a movable frame (near right) and a snap-on rod device (far right) that attaches to the existing closet pole and has holes at different heights to accommodate extra rods.

The full potential of a narrow closet is realized by the installation of a wooden vertical divider and removable shelves. The adult-level clothes rod takes party dresses while the adjustable tension rod below it holds everyday playclothes. The door rack is for beads, bangles, and other accessories.

Play Spaces to Suit Your Child

Children master the world through play; it is their means to discovery and personal development. By creating the right kind of environment, both indoors and outdoors, you can vastly expand your child's possibilities. Although children will play anywhere, they gravitate naturally toward spots that are attractive and option-filled, such as the airy, sunny room at right, in which the four-year-old occupant is happily drawing at a coffee table set aside for her special use. This section of the book will show you ways to create such an environment in your own home—even if your space happens to be limited.

Your efforts in this direction will be well rewarded—expert opinion holds that children who are given opportunities to freely pursue their own interests are more likely to have a positive self-image and an "I can do it!" spirit than children who are pressured to conform to the expectations of others. By allocating age-appropriate play areas inside and outside your home, you will be giving your child an opportunity to explore her potential. And you will be communicating an important message to her: that her play has significance and worth.

Every home and child situation, of course, is unique, so no two play spaces will be exactly the same. But all good play spaces meet certain criteria: they are inviting, they offer challenges, they allow for privacy, and they are safe. Success lies not just in sparking your child's imagination, but also in retaining her interest. With the proper planning, you can achieve this worthwhile goal.

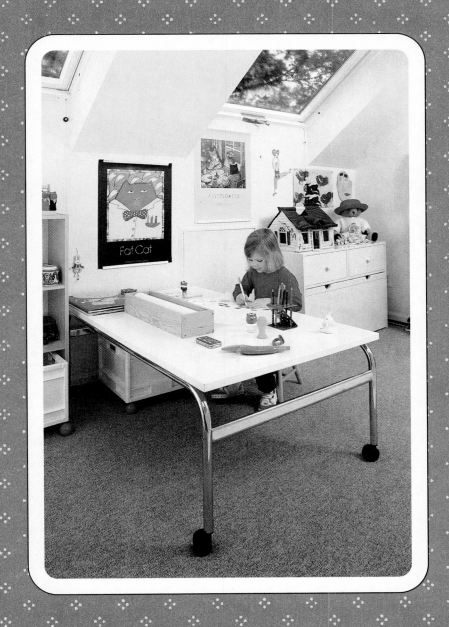

Why Play Environments Matter

Like the work that adults do, children's play deserves full respect. At its best, play represents a delightful fusion of joy with learning. One of its happy outcomes is the development of the total child: physical, social, emotional, and cognitive. But play is by no means automatic. For play's potential to be fully realized, children need opportunities; they must have plenty of space to play in, the right equipment and materials, and sympathetic peers and grownups with whom they can interact. This is why well-constructed and -arranged play spaces are critical to youngsters' all-around growth.

By designating a special play area—even a small area—for your child and thoughtfully arranging her toys and equipment, you foster her concentration, creativity, and experimentation. Your child may know that she is permitted to play in the living room, but if she also knows that there are precious objects, a polished floor, or a special rug that is to be avoided, her play may well be inhibited. By giving her a domain of her own, you contribute to your little one's willingness to try new activities and increase her sense of self.

A separate play area has practical benefits for you, too. It helps control the noise and clutter that necessarily accompany children as they play, permitting you to enjoy a little more peace and quiet—especially on those long rainy or freezing days when outside play is not possible. Under such conditions, a playroom can be not only the welcome answer to the child's needs, but also a godsend for the entire family.

Elements of a good play space

All good play spaces—whether they are inside or outside—have certain features in common. First and foremost, they are inviting, attractive, and full of chances for fun. Plenty of sunshine, good air circulation, and a cheerful atmosphere are important outdoor considerations, although the shadows created by trees are bound to be welcome in the heat of summer. And last, there must be plenty of child-size equipment, as well as abundant opportunities for imaginative play.

The equipment provided should be challenging but not daunting. Each child is unique, and yours will have certain talents and preferences. Some children are daring, others cautious. And some children, especially those with handicaps of one sort or another, have very real and pronounced needs. Observe your youngster as she plays and think about what she likes to do best. What you learn will help you create a play environment for your child that will match her interests and challenge her budding capabilities.

Soaring on her indoor swing, this little girl feels free and powerful. The swing's chains are attached to eyebolts that have been screwed securely into a ceiling beam. Such a swing should be strong enough to support at least twice a child's weight and should be frequently checked for stability and security.

If the play space is to be used by several children, separate it into sections, if possible, to eliminate competition for its resources—a major cause of conflict between preschoolers. Children play more happily if the space is arranged in a way that allows them to move about freely without getting in each other's way and affords them some privacy. Remember to leave room for any playthings your child's friend or friends may bring with them, as well as room for storing her own toys when the fun and games are over.

Physical play is rarely more fun than when carried on outdoors where your child can realize her full energy potential. Still, you should allow space indoors for active undertakings, such as swinging, sliding, or crawling about a small junglegym. Of course, as with yard equipment, you will want to be sure that the pieces are not too high or the floor beneath them too hard in case of a fall. But most youngsters are well adapted to endure some bumps and bruises. Parents who try to protect their child by limiting access to such challenges only postpone essential learning experiences. To run without tripping, to climb easily, to keep one's balance are skills worth a lot to a preschooler— and they become even more valuable at school age.It is better to allow your preschooler to take reasonable risks than to over-protect her in the mistaken belief that she will be better able to handle them when she is older. Parenting, after all, is a role in which you must adopt a long-term view. You often have to weigh current concerns about your youngster's welfare, such as the slight danger of physical harm from active play, against longer-term considerations, such as developing her self-confidence as a physical being and a social one, too. ∴

Making the Most of Indoors

It is never too early in your child's life for you to begin thinking about play spaces. Indeed, you might start when she is still an infant. At this stage, her play consists largely of physical movement and sensory exploration. Since she needs very little room of her own, focus instead on equipment that will enrich her life. An infant seat, for example, will enable her to view the world from a wider vantage point than from floor or crib. A playpen will allow her to amuse herself with rattles and stuffed animals safe from harm. She may also enjoy the additional mobility that walkers, jumpers, and infant swings can give her. But soon she will have outgrown all these. By the time she is about eighteen months old, you will doubtless find yourself looking about your home for a good location for play areas or a playroom.

Creating a playroom

A toddler likes to play near his parents, so at first it pays to choose an area that allows this—a hallway or room off the kitchen or living room, perhaps, where you can keep an eye on

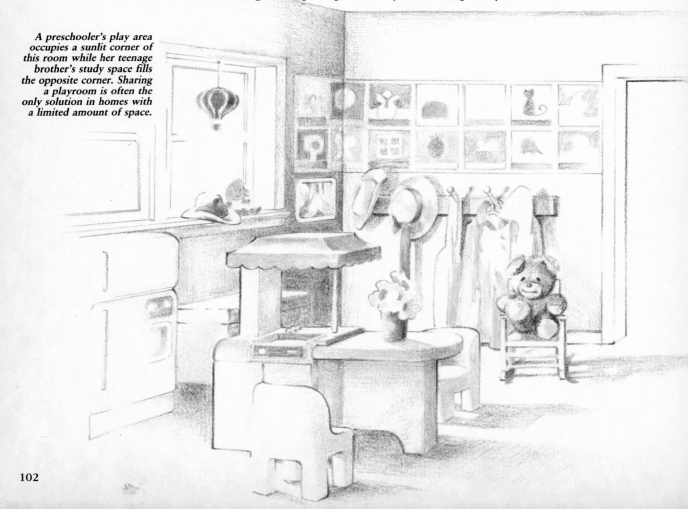

A preschooler's play area occupies a sunlit corner of this room while her teenage brother's study space fills the opposite corner. Sharing a playroom is often the only solution in homes with a limited amount of space.

him and he can see you. When he reaches the age of three or four, he will be more independent and will no longer require constant supervision. You might then consider other spots.

Some families are fortunate enough to have a spare room that lends itself to easy conversion. In an extra bedroom, for instance, you can replace the standard bed with a folding bed, thus freeing up space for play without destroying the room's value as a place for an occasional guest to stay overnight.

Playrooms must be rugged enough to take plenty of wear and tear. Walls and floors will be receiving maximum abuse and should be protected. Prefinished hardboard paneling makes a good wall covering, since it resists dents and scuffing and will not readily pick up crayon, chalk, and fingerprint marks. Paneling is also easy to wash down. You will find a variety of wood patterns and cheery colors to choose from at home centers and lumberyards. If you prefer wallpaper, consider a vinyl-coated paper, because it wears well and cleans easily.

For floors, select a resilient, no-wax covering, preferably made of vinyl, linoleum, or sealed cork that you can mop with soap and water. Or you might opt for a hardwearing carpet or for inexpensive, washable, and replaceable carpet squares. If you use small area rugs on slippery flooring, be sure to put a rubber carpet pad underneath to prevent slipping and other accidents. Low shelves and cupboards and plenty of baskets will make storage easier. To cut down on noise, you might consider installing a sound-absorbent ceiling or hanging heavy drapes.

Whatever you do, make sure that the place you provide for your youngster is entirely safe for him to play in.

Attics and basements can serve as play areas as well, provided your child no longer requires constant supervision. You will want these areas to be clean and cheerful, of course, and free from any toxic materials that might otherwise be stored there. Such spaces have certain advantages: They are often large, underused, and separate from the rest of the house, giving a child the freedom to create both mess and noise without disturbing other family members. But because such areas are generally neglected, they may need extra work to make them secure and comfortable. The basement, for instance, may require a dehumidifier for damp days; the attic, an air conditioner during hot summer months. On the cosmetic side, installing a roof window or skylight will bring sunshine into the attic; painting basement walls a light color and putting down a bright

A cozy play nook was made by redesigning a storage space in a staircase landing. By the addition of a built-in window and ladder, a whole new world was created.

floor covering will help camouflage the drabness of a room below the ground.

What to do when space is limited

Not every house or apartment, of course, is large enough for a child to have her own playroom. But there are plenty of other ways to stretch your space and define special play areas for your child. Building a loft in her bedroom, for example, can produce the effect of a separate playroom: Daytime activities and night-time sleep occur on different levels, making a loft the perfect indoor getaway. For safety's sake, make sure the loft has railings and that the floor beneath it is carpeted.

A play area can also be established in a room that other family members share, especially if the dimensions permit dividing the room with a screen, a curtain, or a removable wall. The partition will allow your child to play freely without infringing on adult space. The side that faces her section can be decorated to suit her; the side that faces the other portion of the room can be hung with items pleasing to you. A bookcase makes another good divider while adding valuable shelf space.

Still another option is to use a room for play during the day, then transform it for evening activities. The dining room is a logical first choice here. You might, for example, have a drop-leaf table set against the wall and put the leaf down during the day to in-crease floor space. In morning and afternoon, with chairs and table against the walls, the child holds sway. At night, toys can be stored in a large closet or in bins on wheels; with the furniture moved back, the dining room regains its adult status.

Finally, consider having several play stations throughout your home. A large closet with the door kept open or an unused fireplace might be equipped as a playhouse; a table in the laundry room can serve for arts and crafts—with the sink's proximity a great advantage. Board games can be played on the floor or on a card table in the living room.

A brother and sister draw on a homemade chalkboard produced by applying a special silicate paint—sold at hardware stores—to a plywood panel.

With endless opportunities for exploration, a versatile climbing gym made of lightweight but sturdy plastic inspires the imagination and exercises the muscles of a toddler. Soft carpeting underneath will cushion any falls and prevent slipping.

When a messy activity is to be carried out, protect the floor or carpeting beneath the table by spreading a sheet of plastic. You might also consider making a folding play screen *(pages 108-109),* which can be transported from room to room and set up to create a child-scaled, individualized play area. Even if you do have a separate playroom, it is still a good idea to establish other spots around the house where a child can keep some toys.

In addition to finding space for a play area, the creation of one involves choosing and arranging equipment carefully. Here, you might take a cue from nursery schools and day-care centers, which group different play stations around the periphery of a room, leaving the center area free. Depending on your child's interests, you might set up one section of the room for painting and drawing, another section for building blocks, another for playing with dolls and stuffed animals, and still another for quiet rest periods. Studies suggest that defined play units such as these invite a youngster to make choices and encourage her to stick with one activity for more than a few minutes at a stretch. Each unit will be more appealing if it is decorated with a special motif and has distinctive furnishings.

Simple, sturdy furniture is practical and can also add to the fun. A set of low, lightweight chairs with a table will find multiple uses. Consider choosing plastic furniture; it will withstand the kind of hard use your child is bound to give it, be easy to move about, and be just as easy to clean. Children love plopping down on large cushions, giant beanbags, and cloth-covered foam-rubber cubes or pillow forms—and your youngster will, too. It will be only a matter of time before her imagination con-

verts these forms into an obstacle course, a mountainous landscape, a tippy tower, a house, or a fort.

Once you have provided the basic furniture, give thought to how the room can be further embellished. A chalkboard will provide a surface for spontaneous art projects and experiments with writing and numbers. A bulletin board or magnetized panel can be used for hanging drawings and other items. And a full-size playhouse, if space permits, will give your child hours of fun.

A well-furnished playroom also includes such fundamental playthings as blocks, dolls, cars, and trucks. An old hat collection or a set of large cardboard boxes that can function as boats, houses, or whatever your little one fancies will enhance make-believe play, so essential to a child's full development. A large roll of brown wrapping paper is a boon to have on hand for art projects: You can pin it up around the perimeter of the room and let your child scribble away to her heart's content. You might also consider buying a collapsible easel that can be propped open for painting and drawing and closed for storage.

In setting up a playroom, remember too that it is important to provide equipment that will allow your youngster to climb, jump, roll, and push, since her urge to actively use her body does not vanish when the sky darkens or the temperature drops and she is forced to play indoors. You have a wide range of equipment to choose from—plastic junglegym, rope ladder, chin-up bar, doorway trapeze, balance beam, or slide. Be sure equipment is safely installed, and check it periodically for soundness to prevent accidents. And put heavy-duty exercise mats or carpets, large cushions, or mattresses around and under climbing equipment to soften falls. The mats will also be put to use for rough-and-tumble play. ⋅:⋅

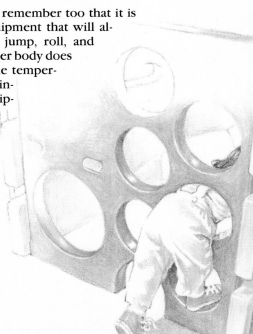

A Fold-Up House

You can use a homemade play screen like the one shown here to transform any open space, either indoors or out, into an instant play area. Although this screen is designed basically as a house, in the imagination of a preschooler it might serve just as well as a puppet theater, a fort, a clubhouse, or a secret hideaway. And, because the screen folds up, moving it about and storing it are easily accomplished.

You can make a similar screen from a four-by-eight-foot sheet of 3/16-inch-thick foam board, found at art-supply stores, or even from corrugated cardboard. For the three walls, slice pieces of the desired size and shape from the sheet with a utility knife, joining them with heavy-duty tape or lacing them together with plastic clothesline, and then cut out doors and windows. Here, only three walls have been provided, with the middle one longer than the sides for greater stability. But by using an additional sheet of foam board, you could cut several more panels for a larger screen and perhaps even a roof. You can use any leftover scraps for shutters or other decorative elements, which may be glued or taped to the panels.

Let your youngster help decorate the completed screen with acrylic or tempera paints, felt markers, and cutouts of colored vinyl-coated paper or shelf paper with sticky backing.

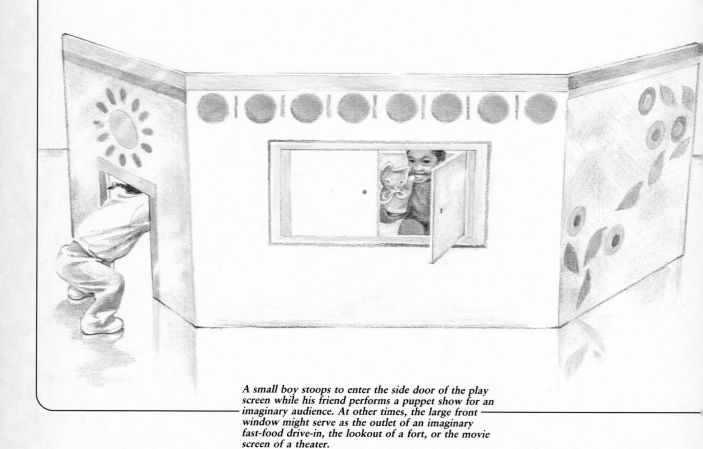

A small boy stoops to enter the side door of the play screen while his friend performs a puppet show for an imaginary audience. At other times, the large front window might serve as the outlet of an imaginary fast-food drive-in, the lookout of a fort, or the movie screen of a theater.

On the inside of the play screen, a little girl grins delightedly at her reflection in a mirror of adhesive reflecting paper. Attaching the paper smoothly can be tricky and is best done by two adults. The wallpaper, curtains, and flowerpot are cut out of colored, adhesive-backed paper and stuck on.

With the addition of a blanket for a roof, the play screen turns into a cozy hideaway. When the children want to seal themselves off from the outside world for make-believe bedtime or to pretend that they are members of a secret club, they can close the shutters.

Turning Your Yard into a Fun Place

When creating outdoor play areas for your child, follow the same principle you would use in planning indoor ones—take the rest of the family's needs into account, along with your child's requirements. You certainly will not want to convert your entire garden into a playground, thus forfeiting the opportunity for you and the rest of your family to enjoy it as a peaceful oasis. But you can reach a compromise that will suit all parties. A well-planned backyard can give your youngster a taste of nature and still provide him with space for play where he can be alone or with friends, for hours at a time. This rich learning environment will greatly enhance his development and his independence.

How to begin

Think first about ways that you can exploit your yard's natural terrain. Look for features that can be used both for active play and for quiet moments. Perhaps you have a garden path that could be resurfaced with soft gravel so that your child could use it for tricycling out of harm's way. Or maybe there is a tall oak tree with a limb strong enough to support an old-fashioned tire swing. If your yard slopes, you might want to fashion a temporary water slide in summer by laying down a sheet of plastic and then rigging up the garden hose so that the water will course down the sheet.

Do not fail to take into account your own needs as you think about the play area. Do you have, for example, a prized vegetable patch or flower bed that you want to keep inviolate? Make sure your youngster understands that

A three-year-old girl pedals her tricycle along a crushed-rock path whose design enhances the landscaping of the family yard while providing her with a regular place to ride. The path's gentle slope and gradual curves give her an exciting challenge without risk of an accident.

he is not to trample through it, uproot the plants, or pick them, no matter how attracted he may be to them.

Planning on paper Drawing a to-scale sketch of your property may help you grasp all the more clearly your yard's possibilities. And since play areas, like playrooms, should evolve as a youngster grows and changes, it makes sense to plan with flexibility in mind. Working on paper, you will be able to arrange equipment for convenience and safety before setting it permanently in place.

Obviously, you will not want to locate a play area near low windows that your child could shatter, or beside a clothesline that he might accidentally run into. Position junglegyms, slides, or other large pieces at least six feet from fences, walls, and the sides of the house. Swings should be set a similar distance, but do take into account the widest arc of a seat in motion so that your child will not hurt himself banging into an obstacle. A sandbox is best located in a sheltered spot, out of the wind, to prevent the sand from blowing about and getting in eyes and ears. A pond or swimming pool should be surrounded by a secure fence with a locked gate and should always be off-limits, except of course when an adult is present. And any garden chemicals and tools should be stored well out of your child's reach. Indeed, you might consider abandoning the use of chemical fertilizers and pesticides while your child is still of an age when he puts things into his mouth indiscriminately.

Follow your preparation of a sketch with a close inspection of the yard. If there are any holes, fill them in to prevent your youngster from twisting an ankle or injuring a knee. And make sure any prickly or poisonous plants and bushes are either fenced off or well away from the section in which he will spend part of each day.

Take into account the play surface. The more resilient it is, the less likely your child will hurt himself in a fall. Sand provides a good cushion but can invite a youngster to dig where he should not be—smack in front of a swing a friend is using, for example. A durable grass, such as Kentucky-31 (a tall fescue used on golf courses), is an excellent choice. Better yet, try mulch. One preferred type is coarsely ground fir bark, which is very soft and splinters less easily than some others. Layer it about six inches deep under and around swings, slides, and climbing equipment, and cover an area of at least five feet with it. To keep the mulch from scattering in dry weather, sprinkle it with the garden hose every day or so.

Making the backyard completely safe, of course, is impossible.

Remember that children have a tendency to set their own limits, minimizing danger to themselves. If you remove the obvious hazards, you can let your child roam and explore without constantly having to follow a step behind.

Your child's input It has been said that for a playground to succeed, its ultimate users must be its builders. While this is not an altogether practical concept, the point is well taken. An essential part of your planning must involve careful consideration of your child's requirements and interests. Talk with him about his wishes, and just as you would in setting up a recreation area indoors for him, observe his spontaneous play outdoors. Chances are, like most preschoolers, he loves to run, swing, balance, and jump, and he enjoys playing with water and sand. But he probably also engages in some form of quiet play. One father, for example, decided to place a sandbox adjacent to a cluster of yews because he noticed that his son liked to spend solitary moments under their shadowy branches. There the boy felt happy and secure, partially hidden from view and absorbed in his own thoughts. For another child, an old packing crate or kitchen cabinet, minus its door and turned on its side, might serve the same purpose as hideaway and retreat.

Before you buy Since children play best in environments that offer challenges and excite their imagination, try to offer as wide a variety of opportunities as possible within the limits of your space. Swings, seesaws, and junglegyms can add immensely to your youngster's enjoyment. Bear in mind, however, that just because you have provided such equipment, you have not necessarily created a playground.

It is not uncommon for a child to pass up an elaborate swing set for a rail fence to climb on. So, too, an old tire may hold hours of fun; it can be rolled, climbed on, sat in, and bounced on. An abandoned crate can become an instant clubhouse.

Before investing good money in equipment, ask yourself some practical questions. How many different ways can your child use the equipment? How soon will he outgrow it? How likely is it to capture and hold his imagination? Can more than one child use the equipment at one time?

Try to include some movable items in the play space that can be rearranged. Most children relish carrying and dragging things about, making and remaking their play areas. A group of four-year-olds, for example, can spend hours carting ordinary boards and boxes from one end of the yard to the other and back again, perhaps to build a house or to lay down a roadway. In the process, the youngsters practice their manual dexterity and use imagination and reason to solve the problem of transportation or construction.

Whatever the equipment you buy, it must, of course, be sturdy and safe. The frames of most modern pieces are wood; make sure they are smooth so there is no risk of abrasions or splinters. Edges and corners should be rounded; bolts recessed or capped. A product safety code has been established to set ideal quality and safety standards for play equipment, but it is voluntary and the manufacturer has the option of following it or not. When purchasing an item, you might want to check with the merchant to see whether the manufacturer has agreed to comply with the product safety code.

Once you have bought and assembled the equipment and put it securely in place, regularly check the nuts and bolts holding the parts together, tightening, lubricating, and replacing them as necessary. Finally, teach your child to use the equipment safely—to stay off wet, slippery rungs and steps and to give moving swings wide berth.

Sandboxes   No play yard would be complete without a sandbox. Sand gives a youngster a chance to dig, pile, sift, and build, and to experiment with a whole range of tools and utensils, from shovels to sieves to funnels. In addition to improving his dexterity, sand exercises his imagination. Dry, sand trickles through small fingers in a soothing fashion. Wet, it can be patted into cakes, buildings, or landscapes or molded into imaginary channels and riverbanks. For a ready water supply, you can place the sandbox near the garden hose.

In buying or building a sandbox, you will want to keep your child's age and size in mind. A toddler will play comfortably in a sandbox about two by four feet; an older child, who will share the box with friends, will need a larger area, one that is about six by six feet. But the sandbox need not literally be a box; it can be shaped in a curve, set in terraces in a hillside, or sunk like a pit into the earth or a patio.

Redwood and cedar are the

This little girl enjoys swaying back and forth and spinning about on an old-fashioned tire swing. Simple, homemade play equipment sometimes offers more opportunities for fun than store-bought items.

113

preferred woods for the box itself, because they weather well. Other types of timber must be treated with preservatives, and you do not want to run the risk of the chemicals' leaching into the sand or possibly being ingested by your child. If the box has a bottom, make holes in it to permit water drainage. (If it lacks a bottom, you might scatter gravel under the sand, unless the sandbox is on high ground that drains well.) Fill the box with coarse, washed sand rather than the builder's variety, which packs too easily. A depth of twelve to eighteen inches will give your youngster sufficient sand to dig in happily. For a six-by-six-foot box, this can amount to more than a ton of sand; so you will want to make arrangements with a supplier to deliver the load. After you have filled the sandbox, keep a few 100-pound sacks of sand in stock to replace what washes or blows away or is otherwise scattered.

Finally, you will need to provide a canvas or plastic cover for the sandbox, in order to protect it from the weather and pollutants and to keep neighborhood cats from using it as a litter box. Some sandboxes have an awning or a roof for shade that can be lowered to cover the sand when the box is not in use.

Swings are another old backyard standby. Indeed, the nineteenth-century Scottish author Robert Louis Stevenson described swinging as "the pleasantest thing a child can do." The heady sensation of flying through the

A scaled-to-size playhouse, sandbox, and slide positioned next to a patio provide these preschoolers with many play possibilities while allowing for easy adult supervision. All the equipment rests on ground covered with grass to cushion accidental falls.

air, seemingly weightless but under control, gives a youngster a very special feeling of freedom and prowess.

A swing can easily be produced from a tire and some rope. If you have a tree or bar to hang it from, suspend the tire from three lengths of rope so it dangles horizontally. This gives your child a comfortable seat, with enough room and support for a friend or two to join him. If you prefer a standard swing, look for one with a seat made of flexible rubber or canvas, which is less likely than metal or wood to injure the youngster who accidentally gets in the way.

How you suspend the swing from limb or frame will, in large part, determine how safe it is for heavy use by your youngster and his friends. While a tire can be hung quite simply, by looping a rope over the tree limb, friction tends to fray the loop, and you will have to check it frequently. A more durable method is to drill a hole through the limb (no harm to the tree) and install a heavy-duty eyebolt, then thread the rope through it. For a swing suspended by chains, you should make sure the S-hooks that attach it to the frame are fully closed; otherwise, you can pinch them shut with pliers, thus eliminating the risk of the chain's disconnecting and spilling the rider to the ground. Or you might check at your hardware store for other options— connector hooks with spring closures, for example. Be sure, too, that the supporting posts of swing sets are anchored in the ground, either with stakes or cement.

Climbing equipment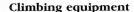 A climbing gym is a versatile plaything—and it will give a youngster the chance to scale heights on his own and build his self-confidence as his prowess grows. It also elicits imaginative play and can become as many things as a child wants it

to be—a rocket to the moon, a castle, or a ship in a raging sea. And climbing teaches spatial relationships—the meanings of up and down, over and under.

A wide variety of commercial climbing equipment is available—dome-shaped junglegyms and pieces with platforms, ladders, ropes, poles, and nets. Slides, too, are for climbing as well as for descending. All such items, for safety's sake, should be firmly anchored in the ground. Parts should be sturdy; you might buy a smaller, good-quality junglegym rather than an elaborate one that is less well-made. And check to see that the steps to the slide have treads, in order to keep little feet from slipping.

Sliding, climbing, and swinging are time-honored childhood activities, as ancient as the simplest and most delightful of all—water play. In

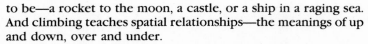

planning your child's play space, take this diversion into account. It will give her hours of fun and learning. Early on she will discover the difference between wet and dry; soon enough she will find that some objects float and others do not. Splashing in a wading pool under your supervision or dashing through a sprinkler will give her much joy, especially when the spray yields a rainbow. Try setting the sprinkler close enough to a swing so your small one gets a gentle shower as she pumps herself back and forth. And what preschoolers do not enjoy a good old-fashioned water fight with full buckets or the hose?

Playhouses and perches

Children also love a playhouse. The structure can be as elaborate as a two-story, wood-and-shingle cottage with doors and windows, or as simple as a sheet that is wrapped around a trio of close-growing trees. In either case, a playhouse will be a place for a youngster to engage in all kinds of pretend play, alone or with companions.

Tree houses are really nothing more than playhouses aloft, although being up high, amid the rustling leaves, adds greatly to their magic. For an aerie such as this, you need a tree with a sturdy trunk that divides quite low into three broad limbs, well away from utility wires. Eight feet is the maximum safe height for such a perch. If you build a tree house for your youngster, be certain that he is ready for it; a child under five years of age is simply too young. And be careful to supervise his play. Attach a sturdy rail to all four sides of the platform and be sure the ladder or stairs are solid. Again, redwood and cedar are good wood choices for outdoor play structures because they resist weathering. When such a house is built on posts rather than in a tree, you should make certain the supports are of treated wood to keep the buried sections from rotting.

Wherever your child's playhouse is located, he will want to furnish it with a few household items—a table and chairs, for example—and bring in toys that are suitable for pretend play. For a tree house, you might want to install a pulley system so he can haul up his toys—or perhaps a lunch basket. Tree house or playhouse, your youngster will regard it as his own domain, and no doubt he will relish the excitement of being in charge. ❖

A child-size kingdom, this homemade play unit has a clubhouse, a sandbox, a bridge, and several ladders. Kits for similar units are sold at hardware stores and toy centers.

117

5 Safety First

Of all the factors to consider when designing your child's living spaces, safety should be the number one priority. This chapter covers protective measures you can take in every room of your home as your child develops the ability to explore more and more of his surroundings on his own. It offers information on fire, water, and electrical hazards and what you can do about these. It also provides many concrete ideas for effective childproofing room by room.

Taking precautions and installing well-chosen safety devices will automatically let the environment say no to your youngster's eager hands even if your back is turned for a moment. The little boy to the right has found, for instance, that the safety latch on a kitchen cabinet will not budge no matter how hard he tries to loosen it. It is important to remember, however, that childproofing will not automatically make your child immune from the thousand little injuries and wounds that mark his rite of passage to maturity. No home is ever 100 percent free of hazards, and not even the most loving and conscientious parent can protect a child against all accidents. But acting reasonably, you can produce an environment that is safe and still fun for your youngster to play and grow in.

Ways to Childproof Your Home

For many parents, home safety measures begin early—even before a child is born—as a natural part of getting ready for the new baby. Merely knowing that your infant is dependent on you for her well-being is a warm motivation for safeguarding your house or apartment; after fixing up the nursery and planning a play space, it is just one step further to implement many of the commonsense safety measures recommended by experts, friends, and your own parents.

As your child's size and mobility increase, her eager quest to explore the world about her intensifies; it is almost impossible to watch over her every minute. Rather than live with unnecessary worry, childproof your home to keep pace with her stages of development. Doing so grants her the freedom she needs to assert her independence and helps protect her against the very real dangers in any dwelling.

Accidents do happen, as the old saying goes, and often they happen to the very young. Household tragedies are the most frequent cause of death among children under fifteen and the leading cause of injury after the first birthday. These facts in themselves should be less cause for fright and more for reasonable vigilance when it comes to your household safety. The hazards in your home require your serious attention, and there are steps you can take to help protect your young one against childhood mishaps. No precautions will prevent all accidents, but the recommendations on the following pages suggest the many things you can do to minimize the possibility of serious injury to your child.

Changing safety needs　　In your infant's earliest months, ensuring his safety will be a fairly simple task. But remember that a newborn infant can wriggle his arms and legs enough to move the few inches that will take him over the side of a bed or other surface. Realizing that such healthy movement can lead to an accident, most parents never leave a child unattended or unsecured on any high surface. Even when strapped into a baby seat, your youngster could topple the seat onto the floor from a tabletop.

In several months your child will be able to roll completely over from his stomach onto his back and vice versa; at this point, special precautions are required to protect him against suffocation. Do not leave pillows in his crib or hang clothing, blankets, or towels over the crib railing, since a young child might inadvertently pull them over his face.

During those gratifying months when your young one begins to creep on his stomach, then to crawl, then to totter along

The Search for Peace of Mind

" When my first child started getting into cabinets, I secured them with rubber bands crossed over the knobs. After several broken nails and one smashed finger, I discovered the cabinet locks that you screw into the inside of the cabinet. Trying to line up the two pieces of these locks required more engineering than I could manage. Fortunately, by the time my second child came along, I found the safety-pin locks that go on the outside of the cabinet knobs. The baby can't get in, but I can. "

" We have some bookcases in my daughter's room. I'm always afraid that she or a friend will try climbing one of them to get something off the top shelf and bring the whole thing down on herself. So I hit on a solution. For the smaller bookcase, I screwed hooks into the wall and threaded fishing line, which is strong but almost invisible, around the upper shelf. For the upper bookcase, my husband used toggle bolts to fix the unit to the wall. "

" I used to have a gate blocking access to the stairs, which was necessary for keeping the babies safe; but I was either catching my hem on it or tripping as I tried to walk over it. Now I have a gate that is a real gate. It is easy to open and to pass through without my having to remove it from the wall. This new gate is really a great idea! "

" Our townhouse has two sets of stairs, so as soon as our son started moving around we taught him how to go down the stairs on his tummy. He became a real speed demon going downstairs and preferred this method well into his threes. He also taught his little sister how to do it. They had the best time bumping down on their tummies, and I never had to worry. "

" One morning at three thirty I was awakened by my two-year-old son, who was standing at the foot of my bed. He was holding an empty plastic pitcher in his hands and repeating the words *Kool-Aid* over and over. Fearing the worst, I went downstairs and discovered that he had poured the drink all over the kitchen floor and on the inside of the refrigerator as he lifted the pitcher off the top shelf. When these nocturnal refrigerator visits continued, I bought a refrigerator lock that is attached with foam tape. He was able to get it open a few times, but then he seemed to lose the knack of opening it or just lost interest, thank goodness. "

" We found that our second child, Joe, had an interest in eating the houseplants and their potting soil—a problem that we never had with his older sister. We decided that the best way for dealing with that was to take the plants to work with us. We'll do without houseplants at home until Joe outgrows this stage. And we learned that you can never be complacent about your children—that one child may get into trouble with something that never interested an older sibling. "

" Like most people, we keep a lot of cleaners, plant foods, and bug killers in the cabinet under the sink. When my son was born I put a childproof latch on the cabinet and a Mr. YUK sticker— that's the symbol for the poison-control phone line—on the outside of the cabinet. As soon as Alex was old enough, I made sure that he knew that the bottles under the sink were poison, and he understood. I never had a problem with his going into that cabinet. "

" When my first child was born, I put childproof latches on all the cabinets and moved anything potentially toxic, like cleaners and medicines, up high. But my husband and I have found that child safety is more of a problem when we visit his parents. Since they don't have small children, their house is not childproofed. When we come over, my mother-in-law puts their cleaning products and medicines, which they usually keep below the sink, in a box that they put on top of their dresser. We also had to be very careful over there when our little girl was around one year old because she didn't know how to negotiate stairs, and their stairs are very steep. "

" I think nightstands and coffee tables can be the most dangerous items to have in a household with children. Unfortunately, my wife and I had to learn this the hard way. When our son Danny was about two and climbing all over the place, he managed to get up on the sofa and fall onto our glass-topped coffee table. He got a nasty gash on the mouth and we had to make a trip to the emergency room for stitches. We sold the coffee table, but a few years later he fell out of bed at four in the morning and cut his cheek on the sharp-edged nightstand. Why we didn't have enough sense to move the nightstand after the incident with the coffee table is beyond me. "

121

holding onto the furniture, and finally to walk unsupported, his ever-increasing mobility will demand vigilance on your part. As you well know, a child makes full use of the floor once he begins crawling. Add to this teething and his newfound urge to pick up and chew on everything in sight, and your task of thoroughly childproofing your home from the floor up becomes evident. Regularly check coffee tables, floors, and other low surfaces to keep them free of thumbtacks, coins, marbles, and other small objects that your baby might swallow or choke on. Also keep edibles such as popcorn and hard candies out of your little one's reach, since they pose a serious choking hazard. Take care to cap all unused electrical sockets with plastic safety plugs. And you should never leave fans, heaters, humidifiers, portable TVs or radios, or other electrical appliances on the floor where your baby can get to them.

Teaching good habits

As your little one grows into a toddler and a preschooler, you can begin to educate her to protect herself. Keeping your explanations simple, you can start by giving her one-word warnings, such as "Hot!" as you prevent her from touching a stove burner or a steaming serving dish. Fortunately, at this stage, she will have begun to try to imitate you—the important grownup in her life. She will pay as much or more attention to what you do as to what you say, noticing your care when handling hot cooking pots, using tools, and dealing with electrical appliances and other potentially hazardous household items. Treat such objects with the same healthy respect you expect your child to use; especially resist the temptation to amuse a young child with the flame from a brightly colored cigarette lighter. Blurring the distinction between tools and toys will weaken your attempts to teach a consistent safety message.

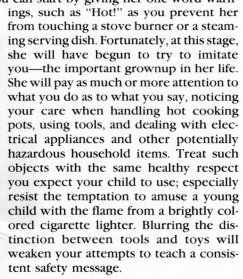

While you should encourage basic safety habits in your child early, he may be too young to know when he has ventured into dangerous territory. Many parents find safety gates useful to demarcate safe

With her free arm, this mother easily swings open the pressure-mounted gate at the top of several steps. For a full stairway, a hardware-mounted gate is most secure.

space for a child. You can put them in your kitchen and dining room doorways and easily watch your youngster while you prepare dinner. Installed on stairways, they can provide special protective barriers to keep a young child from unsupervised play on the steps. Do not use wooden accordian-style gates manufactured before 1985, however. If you are given one of this date or earlier, discard it. Such gates have caused head entrapment, injury, and fatalities. The spaces between slats or bars on the new accordian gates are a maximum of two and three-eighths inches apart to prevent a child from wedging his head in them.

Before your child is able to climb onto windowsills to gaze on the wide world, install burglar latches to prevent his little hands from opening the windows. If you possibly can, develop the habit of opening windows at the top rather than at the bottom when you need to get fresh air. And especially in his early years, secure any drawer or cabinet containing dangerous objects or toxic substances with a childproof latch. Simple, effective plastic latches are available at many hardware stores. They are quick and easy to install, cause minimum inconvenience to adults who have to open them, and provide you with great peace of mind while they protect your child's health and life.

The spring mechanism on the drawer safety latch above lets parents open the drawer by depressing the latch. The simple cabinet latch below, mounted with four screws inside the cabinet, is similarly easy for adults to operate, while allowing children to open the cabinet only a few inches.

Fire prevention

Among the home safety precautions that you will wish to consider, fire prevention should rank high. As a leading cause of accidental home fatalities, fire poses a real danger that should not be underestimated, especially when you have an infant or a small child to consider. Fortunately, you can take many measures both to minimize the danger of a fire's occurring and to help your family survive in the event that a fire does break out.

Where there's smoking, there's danger

A great many fires result from careless smoking; a lighted cigarette dropped onto bedding or upholstered furniture may smolder for hours, creating smoke that can suffocate or be fatally toxic even before the flames erupt. If there are no smokers in your household, and if you make nonsmoking a rule for your baby-sitters, your child's risk is substantially reduced. But if smoking is a fact of life in your home, do everything you can to promote safe smoking practices. No one should ever smoke in bed or even when stretched out drowsily on a couch after a few drinks or a long day's work. Use deep, wide-rimmed ashtrays and place them flat on a table, never on a lap or on the arm of an upholstered chair or sofa. No adult smoker should ever leave matches or lighters where children can reach them.

More than 150 people a year die in fires caused by children playing with lighters, and many others are burned. Although it may seem unlikely, even a two-year-old can manipulate a cigarette lighter and unwittingly start a deadly fire.

In the winter months, kerosene and space heaters can present major household fire hazards. If you use one of these, carefully follow the manufacturer's instructions; you can obtain further information by writing to the Consumer Product Safety Commission, Washington, D.C. 20207, and asking for its product fact sheet on heaters. Store fuel for your heater in a safe place—preferably an outdoor shed or a garage area with a childproof lock—and place the heater in a spot where your child will not knock it over while playing. Keep a space heater away from kitchen and bathroom areas, and to avoid the possibility of electrocution, never allow your young one to touch it, especially with wet hands. Use a kerosene heater only in a properly ventilated space and be sure to position any heater well clear of drapes, furniture, and other flammable objects. Most important, always turn a heater off before the family goes to sleep.

If you have a wood stove or fireplace in your home, screen it off securely and teach your child the importance of not coming too close. Know also that it is inviting disaster to leave a child alone in a room with a fire burning in the fireplace. Since wood stoves can get very hot, you may wish to postpone using one in your home until your youngster knows enough to protect herself. In any case, burn only safe materials, such as firewood, to keep noxious fumes from developing. It is also important to have your flue cleaned annually to prevent a flammable buildup that might lead to a chimney fire.

Sometimes, in spite of the best of precautions, a home fire does flare up. If you discover it early, you may be able to extinguish a small fire yourself. Lacking an extinguisher, you can smother a stovetop grease fire with a pot lid or douse it with salt or baking soda. Do not use water, which will only spread the blaze. If a fire has already produced great clouds of smoke or looks too big for you to put out quickly, clear the whole family from the house and call the fire department from a neighbor's phone. Many

During a family fire drill, this five-year-old practices climbing down an escape ladder. Store your ladder under the bed or in the closet, and stress that it is for emergency use only.

families keep a fire extinguisher at hand; if you purchase one, store it out of your child's reach but where you can get at it readily and recharge it periodically.

To protect your family against fires that break out at night, install smoke detectors; be sure those you install sound a warning loud enough to wake everyone from a deep sleep. Test your detectors regularly, and keep them supplied with fresh batteries if they are the type requiring them. It is also important that you hold regular family fire drills and practice two escape routes, in case one is blocked by smoke or flames. If your home is more than one story high, you may have to install escape ladders as part of your fire safety plan. If you live in an apartment building, be sure to instruct your youngster not to use the elevators in the event of a fire.

It is wise to begin explaining fire safety to your child when she is young. A toddler or preschooler may think that she can seek protection from fire by crawling into small play spaces or under a table, where it is difficult or impossible for parents or fire fighters to reach her quickly; teach her that she should always escape from the house rather than hide from a fire. Since more fire deaths are caused by smoke inhalation than by burning, make sure your child knows that the best air in a burning building is near the floor. When practicing your family escape routes, you can show her how to crawl to safety.

Always buy flame-resistant sleepwear for your child, and wash the garments in detergent, not soap, to preserve their retardant qualities. Make certain that your child understands that if her clothing does catch fire, she should not run but should cross her arms over her chest and cover her face with her hands, then drop to the floor, and roll back and forth to smother the flames. You can make a game out of practicing this lifesaving "stop, drop, and roll" technique.

Most young children will inevitably display curiosity about the many electrical appliances, cords, and outlets around the house; however, a few simple measures will help you protect your child from accidental shocks and burns. For one thing, you should never leave any appliance plugged in and unattended where your child can get at it.

A crawling infant may think that wall sockets are the perfect size for his probing little fingers. Install outlet caps or full outlet shields in any

A child practices the "stop, drop, and roll" technique taught to schoolchildren through the National Fire Protection Association's "Learn Not to Burn" program. Your fire department can arrange a school presentation or help you to teach fire safety at home.

sockets near the floor; be sure prongs on all plugs are inserted fully into wall sockets to reduce the chance of their being pulled out by a child.

And since an electrical cord may be taken for a long, flexible teething device, keep cords as much out of sight and reach as possible. Hospitals treat numerous infants each year for mouth burns that occurred when the children chewed on extension cords. Hide cords behind furniture, but make sure that the furniture does not pinch the cord and cause it to fray; you may also use electrician's tape to keep cords flush against walls or baseboards. Inspect all cords regularly for fraying. Discontinue use of any appliance with a frayed or worn cord at once and have the cord replaced.

Early on, introduce your child to the basics of electrical safety, laying special stress on the dangers posed by the combination of electricity and water. Keep electrical appliances out of the bathroom and away from the kitchen sink. Also tell your child never to touch a kitchen appliance with wet hands or while standing on a wet patch of floor.

If your child does receive an electrical shock, you need to help him without shocking yourself as well. If you can do it quickly, turn off the current with the master switch in your fuse box to shut off all household power. If you cannot do that, move him out of contact with the electrical current without touching him. If you touch him with your bare hands, or even with a pair of thin rubber gloves, the current from his body will shock you as well and render you powerless to help. Stand on something dry and nonconducting, such as a rubber mat, folded blanket, or thick wad of newspaper, and use a rope, wooden pole, or some other dry, nonmetallic object to separate your child from the source of the electrical shock; if that fails, try to pull from the wall socket the plug of the piece of equipment that is shocking him, using a nonmetallic object. Then call at once for medical help. In moments of emergency you will want to know as much as possible about cardiopulmonary resuscitation and first aid for burns, so study these subjects before the need arises.

Water poses some special dangers for a young child, not only in combination with electricity but also by itself. Always test your youngster's bathwater temperature with your elbow or the inside of the wrist, which is more sensitive than your hand, before putting him in the tub. As an added safety measure, set the temperature control on your water heater no higher than 125 degrees to avoid scalding; you may have to call a service

Swivel plates (top), plastic plugs (middle), and permanent outlet covers (bottom) help prevent electric shock by keeping children from inserting metal objects or their fingers into wall sockets.

Holiday Safety Tips

For parents and child alike to enjoy fully the high spirits associated with the various holidays, a few special measures are necessary to help ensure your youngster's safety. Remember that a young child can easily get bored or tired—and suffer little accidents—while you are distracted preparing for an elaborate family gathering or putting up holiday decorations. See if you can arrange for a family member or neighbor to help keep your little one happily occupied until the majority of the preparations are over.

Around Thanksgiving and the different religious holidays, the kitchen becomes even more of a focal point than usual. For everyone's safety, make sure your oven is in good working order to avoid overheating, and keep the stovetop cleared of any fat-filled pans. Put electric knives, blenders, or mixers away as soon as you are through with them. After holiday parties, remove glasses and ashtrays from low surfaces; ingesting alcohol can be fatal for a young child. And you should always check wastebaskets, seat cushions, and upholstery for dropped ashes, to prevent a late-night fire.

For families that celebrate Christmas, household safety should start with the Christmas tree. If your child is very young, you may wish to purchase a tabletop tree, to keep it out of her reach. For a large tree, either cut your own or be sure to buy a moist, fresh one; a dry tree that catches fire may ignite an entire room. To test a tree for freshness, pick it up and sharply thump the base on the ground. Needles will cascade off a dry, old tree. Once at home, stand the tree in a base that can be filled with water. Check the water level daily and add more water as needed to keep the tree from drying out. If you prefer to buy an artificial tree for your home, make sure that it is fire-resistant.

Whether natural or artificial, your tree should be located away from a fireplace, heating units, and exits. Place any decorations with removable parts, metal, or glass on high branches of the tree; use soft, nonbreakable decorations attached with ribbons or yarn on lower tree limbs that your youngster can reach. Refrain from using ornaments that your child might mistake for candy or edibles. Check any tree-light sets—both old and new—for loose ends, broken bulbs, frayed wires, or cracked plugs; to avoid socket overload, use no more than three sets of lights on an extension cord.

Many common Christmas items can be poisonous to children, and you will want to be careful about where you place these. Holly and mistletoe berries, tinsel that contains lead, and the salts used to produce bright colors in a fire are all toxic. Keep them out of your child's reach.

Anytime you plan to use fireworks or fire, on Independence Day for example, take precautions. Store fireworks in a locked garage or shed, not in the house, and under no circumstances should you allow younger children to play with them. Even older children should be supervised when using fireworks. Never place combustible decorations or cornstalks near a stove, candle, or other heat source. And bear in mind that while Fourth of July sparklers may be pretty to look at, they burn at extremely high temperatures and their metal rods can ignite clothing easily.

representative to change the setting. Some water heaters come preset at 140 or 150 degrees; thus, you may need to request a lower temperature. To double-check the setting, wait about an hour after you have changed it, then put a cooking thermometer in a glass, run hot water in the glass for several minutes, and check the reading.

It is often advisable to bathe a small baby in the kitchen sink or in a small plastic tub rather than in an adult-size bathtub to avoid mishaps. You can set a plastic baby tub in the bathtub and fill it directly from the tap there. If you do bathe your child in the family bathtub, turn the taps off before putting him in it; this prevents flow from the hot faucet from raising the water temperature while the bath is in progress. Be sure to keep your baby well away from the faucet so that he does not needlessly bang his head. You may want to take the added precautions of covering the faucet with a rubber protector and running some cool water through the faucet to cool off the metal before putting your child in the tub. So that your baby will not slip while you bathe him, use a rubber mat or install nonslip tape or friction decals on the bottom.

The basic rule of water safety is never to leave your child alone in the bathtub, even for a few seconds. A child can drown quickly in as little as two inches of water. So make sure that you have all the necessary bathtime equipment with you before you begin bathing your youngster; this way you will not have to go off in search of anything. Either ignore the doorbell and telephone during his bath or lift your child out of the tub, wrap him up, and take him with you.

As your child grows, you can employ tried-and-true methods in virtually every room of your home to make the doors, windows, furniture, and floor coverings safer. Begin by checking furniture to make sure every piece is heavy and sturdy enough so that she cannot pull any over on herself. Also look for sharp corners on coffee tables and other low pieces that a toddler might run into. Cover all dangerous corners and edges with protective guards to help your child avoid painful bumps and bruises. To provide secure footing, attach all area rugs to the floor or use nonslip backing. If you have runners or carpeting on stairways, make sure it is firmly tacked in place and check it regularly to prevent your youngster from tripping on the steps.

Allowing a young child maximum physical freedom around the house is probably an almost impossible goal to achieve; however, as he grows, you can at least limit his explorations to rooms or places that you feel are relatively safe. To help keep your youngster out of dangerous areas, you may wish to use spring-loaded, self-closing hinges, and pneumatic or hydraulic door closers that shut doors automatically. One self-closing hinge per door is usually enough to do the job; more will cause the door to close too hard, with a loud and dangerous slam. Door locks are available in several styles, such as barrel bolt, pivot, safety chain, and hook-and-eye; these special locks will baffle a small child's attempts to undo them, but they will allow

The plastic doorknob sleeve spins in this child's hand as he tries to open the door. A firm adult grip will open the door easily.

older children to open the door in case of an emergency.

For a sliding door you can install a bar that flips down into a horizontal position to wedge the door shut. You can also drill holes to insert rivets or nails where the two metal frames of the sliding doors overlap at the center when the door is closed.

If you wish to keep a young child from turning a doorknob, cover the knob with a plastic safety sleeve. Some doors have push-button locks, which can be dangerous if they enable a child to lock himself in his room or in the bathroom. You can unscrew knobs of this kind and either replace them with nonlocking knobs or reverse them so that the lock is on the other side of the door. For additional peace of mind, you might want to install an alarm that lets you know when your child has opened a particular door. You can rig a small bell on the door, or you can put in an electronic alarm that sounds whenever someone touches the doorknob or breaks a magnetic contact between the door and its frame.

Safeguarding windows   To prevent your child from opening windows, arrange furniture so that there is no easy way for her to climb onto windowsills. If your child does manage to reach a window, however, a grille is even more effective than a screen as a barrier against falling out. You can lock a window with an ordinary sash lock or with a more secure key lock. If you choose the latter option, be sure to hang the key near the window, where a small child cannot get at it, but where adults and older children can reach it if the window will be used in the event of a fire. If you are sure that a particular window will never be used as an emergency exit, you can fasten the bottom half shut or install a block of wood in one of the tracks so the window cannot be raised. With the bottom half fastened shut, it is still possible to open the top half of the window to let in air. A sliding window, like a sliding door, can be secured with a bar, or with a metal clip that blocks its track. To stop a child from opening a casement window, remove the crank and store it out of reach or immobilize the crank by wiring it to the latch.

Broken glass can also be a serious hazard when you have an active child around, so use safety glass for all windowpanes or door panels within eighteen inches of the floor. Your local building inspector is the best source of safety-glass information. To prevent your child from rushing into floor-length windows and glass doors, arrange furniture to block access or decorate the glass with a few colorful decals so he will not mistake the clear glass for an unobstructed opening. ⋅⋅⋅

A Room-by-Room Guide to Child Safety

Parents seasoned by the trials of experience report one common safety lesson when it comes to children: It is all too easy to underestimate an infant's ability to move about once he begins to crawl. Unprepared for a child's rapid development, a parent may unexpectedly discover him piling up stuffed animals to vault out of a crib or using a bookshelf as a ladder to reach an open window. Rather than trying to anticipate what territory might next appeal to their avid explorer, many parents find it worthwhile to childproof the home room by room. Along with minimizing obvious dangers, this spares worry about accidental damage to any valuable items or keepsakes.

The living room   In all likelihood, your child will spend a good deal of time with the family in the living room; it is only natural for her to want to bask in the attention of the family or to play while others talk, read, listen to music, or watch television. With a few adaptations, your living room or family room can become a less likely spot for your youngster or your furnishings and other possessions to come to harm.

Expensive electronic equipment—a television set or a stereo—represents a source of mystery to a curious young child, who may even want to get inside it to discover the source of the pictures and sound. If possible, you should conceal all such appliances within cabinets; to prevent overheating, make sure that there are a few inches of air-circulation space in the cabinet. Otherwise, locate these against the wall and tape down wires and cables with tough, clear packing tape.

The cords from your lamps require the same treatment as television and stereo wires; for that matter, the use of lamps necessitates careful planning. A child can easily pull over a floor lamp or a top-heavy table lamp, an accident that can jerk the plug from its socket and shatter the bulb. For maximum safety, use only ceiling fixtures and wall-mounted lights. If it is impossible to eliminate floor and table lamps, position

A protective shortener hides the cord of this table lamp. Since it does not trail on the floor, a child will be less likely to grab it, trip over it, or chew on it.

them with their cords taped securely to the floor or baseboard. If a bulb burns out and you lack a replacement for it, you should either leave the dead bulb in place or unplug the lamp; a child may otherwise poke his finger in the empty socket and receive an unpleasant shock.

Bookshelves and display cases

Books appeal mightily to young children; their pages seem made for scrawling, drawing, and tearing. If you have books that you particularly cherish, you may wish to put them in a secure place for a few years. You may also consider installing wall-hung shelves out of your youngster's immediate reach. If you use freestanding bookcases rather than wall-hung shelves, you need to protect a child from pulling over one of these once he unloads its contents. You can improve the stability of this type of bookcase by fastening it to wall studs with screws. Bookcases with cabinet doors tend to discourage a youngster from climbing; and wedging books tightly on the shelves makes the books harder for small hands to pull out.

Similar considerations apply to a china cabinet or any other display case you may have. If a cabinet is not built into the wall or screwed securely in place, make sure that its center of gravity remains low by not overloading the top shelves; any top-heavy cabinet is more likely to be tipped over accidentally. To reduce a child's temptation to climb up a prized cabinet, keep the doors locked or secured with a childproof safety latch and consider storing your treasures out of reach or even out of sight until your child is older.

The dining room

Your youngster will undoubtedly find occasion to venture into the dining room, so inspect tables and floors periodically for general safety. Especially avoid leaving a tablecloth in place at any time after a meal. A toddler may merely tug on a cloth to balance herself, pulling down dishes, centerpieces, and anything else on the table in the process. Keep chair seats tucked underneath the table to reduce the possibility that your child might use a chair as a stepladder to climb onto the table. If a liquor cabinet is within reach of her hands, keep the doors locked or safety-latched. Not only are liquor bottles heavy and breakable, their contents can be fatal to your child if ingested.

The kitchen

More accidents probably occur in the kitchen than in any other part of the house, especially just before breakfast and dinner, when meals are being prepared and the entire family is rushing about. Thus it is never too early in your youngster's life to begin childproofing this potentially dangerous room; by the time he starts to explore on his own, your safety measures will provide him with a modicum of protection.

First and foremost, realize that you cannot predict your toddler's movements; you may warn him not to run in the kitchen, but you cannot keep him from bumping into things. Cover any sharp edges on kitchen counters with soft plastic guards. By the same token, you cannot control his ambitious desire to touch every item that catches his eye. Even before you think it necessary, keep appliances, cooking utensils, and all breakable items away from the edges of your counters. When loading silverware into a dishwasher or dish drainer, always put sharp points downward. When dishes are done, immediately dry and place knives and any other harmful objects where they belong.

Childproofing features in this family's kitchen include safety latches on the oven and refrigerator, pots on back burners with handles turned out of reach, and plastic sleeves on the dials that control the oven and the stovetop burners.

As early as possible, teach your child to respect your stove or microwave—or both—and never to assume either is safe for her to touch. While you are cooking, warn her away from the stove area so that she will not be burned by accidental spills or by the spattering of hot oil. You can install guard rails to fence in your stovetop, but do not rely on these barriers alone for protection. Always keep cooking-pot han-

dles pointed toward the center of the stove, since your child may grab them and cause a scalding spill or you may accidentally knock against them or catch them with your sleeve; it is also wiser to cook on back burners whenever possible since front burners are more accessible to a young child's eager hands. For an added touch of security with an easy-to-open or loose oven door, you can buy a special lock that will keep little hands from opening it. Never store items—especially cookies and candies—that might have an appeal to your youngster in cabinets that are located over the stove. She might burn herself trying to climb up to fetch them.

Medium-size appliances, such as microwaves, toaster ovens, and other countertop kitchen devices should be located well beyond your child's reach; observe all normal safety precautions. If you must heat baby food or bottles in a microwave, be aware that the contents may be scalding hot even if the container is cool enough to touch; experts generally advise against using the microwave for this purpose. Always mix or shake heated food or drink first and test it on the inside of your wrist before giving it to your little one.

You may wish to install a special lock on the refrigerator to prevent unsupervised rummaging by your youngster. It is a good idea to label any potentially confusing items so that a baby-sitter does not, for example, mistake a pitcher of martinis for a harmless container of ice water. If you use refrigerator magnets, avoid hand-painted ones that may have been colored with potentially toxic lead paint. Buy larger magnets that your child cannot put in her mouth; keep them high on the refrigerator door where she cannot get at them.

Toxic substances and trash

Some safety experts recommend that you place all hazardous substances in an unreachable, locked cabinet. At the very least, keep locks or childproof latches on any kitchen drawer or cabinet with potentially dangerous contents. This includes the cabinets where you store cleaning compounds, insecticides, and other toxic products; drawers full of sharp knives; and cupboards containing heavy casserole dishes or mixing bowls.

If the telephone or doorbell rings while you are using a toxic product such as floor polish or window cleaner, you should pick your child up and carry her with you. Leave any potentially toxic substance in its original container so you can consult the label and know what to do should poisoning occur despite your precautions. An index card by the phone should include your local poison-control center's number, as well as the telephone

---

Kitchen Items to Keep Away from Children

Below is a listing of common kitchen items that can be hazardous to small children. Store them—and any other potentially dangerous material specific to your household—in cabinets with child-proof latches or on shelves well out of reach. Use the original containers with labels, and when possible, safety lids.

- ammonia
- copper, brass, and silver polish
- cleansers, for the sink, floor, drain, and oven
- dishwashing detergents and hand soaps
- floor wax
- food extracts
- furniture polish
- hand lotions
- knives, apple corers, and potato peelers
- lighters and lighter fluid
- matches
- plastic bags and wraps
- roach repellents
- scissors
- scouring pads
- spices
- vitamins

numbers of your pediatrician, two neighbors, and the nearest emergency medical service.

Since children will also explore the trash can, if given a chance, your kitchen refuse can or wastebasket should also be securely covered. Teach your child early that rubbish containers are not playthings; at the same time, take particular care with broken glass, discarded razor blades, sharp-edged can lids, or other hazardous items that a child might find while fishing through the garbage. Wrap such potentially dangerous items carefully and hide them under other discards. If your kitchen has a trash compactor or garbage disposal, you should either secure the control switches with locking covers or replace them with key-operated switches. Be sure to keep the keys well out of your youngster's reach.

Stairs and hallways

No matter what their age, children seem to regard staircases as great challenges—something to mount and descend, again and again. Teach your toddler to hold on to the banister, to walk— not run—up or down the stairs, and to pick up toys left on them after play. Always keep stairs well lighted so that she will be able to see where she is going.

Fully carpeting a staircase will reduce the chance of a child's slipping on steps. By the same token, a hallway carpet at the top of a staircase will prevent slips and make a tumble down the stairs less likely. Tack down any stair and hall carpeting securely, so your child cannot accidentally or deliberately pull tacks loose; check the carpeting regularly for frayed or worn spots that could trip small feet.

Safety gates are essential at the top and bottom of any stairway used by your child. You might want to install the gate two or three steps up from the bottom to allow a crawling infant a few steps to play on and to practice climbing skills. You can pressure-mount a gate at the bottom of a flight of stairs, but at the top of the stairs be sure to use a more secure hardware-mount to prevent a child from knocking the gate loose and taking a bad tumble. Just as the slats of a safety gate should be no more than two and three-eighths inches apart, so, too, should the posts, or balusters, of a handrail. If your posts have gaps wide enough for a child's head or body to squeeze through, you can have a piece of clear acrylic plastic cut to fit and secured against the railings to serve as a transparent barrier.

The bathroom

Your child's natural inquisitiveness will make it necessary for you to exercise special vigilance in protecting him from bathroom hazards. Since children find ingenious ways to explore drawers and bathroom cabinets, always keep these locked or safety-latched; never leave medicines, razors, or toiletry items lying in plain sight after use, and always throw away medicines that you no longer need.

Water also poses a special danger to a young child, who may find the toilet and bathtub fixtures—and their contents—fascinating. You may wish to install a safety latch on your toilet to prevent the possibility of a child's drowning or of the lid's falling on his head; in addition, always drain the tub when a bath is finished to avoid the hazard of standing water. As mentioned already, an infant can even tumble into a diaper pail and drown, so take the precaution of equipping yours with a childproof lid or safety latch.

A wet and slippery floor can cause nasty falls and head injuries. Keep plenty of paper towels on hand in the bathroom and show your child how to soak up spilled or splashed water with them; a strategically located bath mat can absorb some of the water, but choose one with nonslip backing. Because your youngster will often be barefoot in the bathroom, thoroughly sweep up any broken glass immediately after an accident and use plastic, metal, or paper cups rather than glass ones in order to guard against breakage.

It is highly recommended by safety experts that you avoid using electrical appliances when your child is in the bathroom, since the presence of water makes it a household location especially conducive to electrical shocks. If you have to use appliances here, consider installing a ground fault circuit interrupter (GFCI). A GFCI does not prevent shock altogether, but it does cut off the electricity flowing through the person handling the appliance.

Finally, it is best to remove bathroom locks or replace them with those that can be opened from the outside when your child is very young.

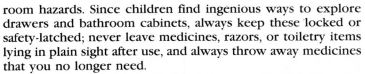

A medicine-cabinet latch in this childproofed bathroom keeps razors, pills, and other dangerous items inaccessible to children; a toilet latch guards against drowning accidents.

Bathroom Products to Secure

Family bathrooms commonly contain cosmetics, medications, and cleaning agents that are harmful if ingested, as well as grooming implements that can cause nasty cuts if used improperly. Make sure that your medicine cabinet is childproof and that the following items are located in spots that are inaccessible to your child.

- aerosol sprays
- aftershave lotions, perfumes, and colognes
- birth-control pills
- bubble-bath soap and bath oils
- cleaning and scouring agents
- corn and wart removers
- eyeliners and mascara
- hair sprays, shampoos, gels, and dyes
- laxatives
- manicure and pedicure implements
- nail polish and remover
- permanent-wave solution
- prescription and nonprescription medicine
- toothpaste and mouthwash
- witch hazel or rubbing alcohol

Knocking before entering the bathroom when your youngster is using it can serve to protect his privacy needs.

Garage and yard   The need for childproofing extends beyond the doors of your home and encompasses your garage, toolshed, and yard—all areas that may need adapting as your young one begins to explore and expand her world.

Your garage, basement, workshop, or any other area where you keep such adults-only items as tools and dangerous chemicals should be securely locked. Unplug power tools not in use and store any hazardous items in locked cabinets or hang them high on the wall where your child cannot reach them. Hang sharp tools high on wall-mounted spring clips.

Take similar precautions with potentially hazardous adult recreational equipment. Lawn darts, for example, should always be kept under lock and key; fishing hooks, with their bright lures, should be stored where a child cannot get at them.

Use only specially designed safety cans for storing flammable liquids, and install smoke detectors in any area where you keep them. You should throw away chemicals you are finished with, as well as any rags that have been soaked in flammable or otherwise hazardous liquids. Call your community's landfill or public works department to obtain information on safe disposal of hazardous chemicals.

An aid to automobile safety

While driving, this mother uses an adjustable swivel mirror attached to her car's visor to keep an eye on her child, who is securely strapped into a car seat. The additional mirror eliminates the risk of turning around constantly to check on the child, who is safer riding in the car's back seat.

Teach your child not to play in the driveway, especially near garage doors. If your garage has roll-up doors, stress to your youngster the importance of keeping her fingers away from the roller channels and the gaps between the panels. For added protection against pinched fingers, use rubber cushioning strips to buffer the gaps. Even if you have a pressure-sensitive automatic door opener that stops the door if it hits a solid object, teach your child that running under a closing door is an unacceptable game; also, make sure that the switch is well out of her reach and that the remote-control device kept in the car is inaccessible to her. Test automatic doors regularly to make sure they are functioning properly.

Making your yard a safe place

If you work in the yard with such tools as hedge clippers and sharp-edged gardening implements, keep them away from your child and avoid leaving her alone with them. Make sure she stays at a safe distance while you are mowing the lawn, and always remove the key from a riding mower. Put safety covers on all outdoor electrical outlets, and close the covers as soon as you have finished using power tools.

To prevent your young one from getting into trash cans in your yard or tipping them, consider running a stout elasticized cord under each lid handle and hooking it onto the side handles. By installing hooks next to your trash cans and using additional cords to hold the containers against a shed or garage wall, you can keep them from being knocked over.

Your child's outdoor play area

Before allowing your child full run of the yard, search it as thoroughly as she will in play. Poke around underneath bushes and in other out-of-the-way corners and check for such hazards as rusty nails and broken glass and cigarette butts. In the summer months, be on the lookout for mushroomlike fungus growths that can spring up overnight on your lawn. And you should familiarize yourself with poisonous or irritating plants and eliminate any of them from your garden.

If your property has any abandoned wells or shallow depressions in the ground, have them filled in and covered. Install four-sided fencing with self-latching, self-closing gates around a swimming pool; the latch should be above a child's reach. Also fence off any dangerous areas of your yard, such as ponds, hot tubs, and patches of thorny shrubbery. With these precautions, a child will still need supervision in those vulnerable early years, but you will be able to rest assured that you have created a safer place for him to enjoy. ∴

Bibliography

BOOKS

Aaron, David, *Child's Play*. New York: Harper & Row, 1965.

Ames, Louise Bates, *He Hit Me First*. New York: Dembner Books, 1982.

Arena, Jay M., M.D., and Miriam Bachar, *Child Safety Is No Accident*. Durham, N.C.: Duke University Press, 1978.

Barnes, Bill, *Building Outdoor Playthings for Kids*. Blue Ridge Summit, Pa.: Tab Books, 1985.

Barnes, Joanna, *Starting from Scratch*. New York: Hawthorn Books, 1968.

Beckwith, Jay, *Make Your Backyard More Interesting Than TV*. New York: McGraw-Hill Book Co., 1980.

Beebe, Brooke McKamy, *Best Bets for Babies*. New York: Dell Publishing Co., 1981.

Behme, Robert Lee, *The Outdoor How-to-Build-It Book*. New York: Hawthorn Books, 1971.

Berends, Polly Berrien, *Whole Child/Whole Parent*. New York: Harper & Row, 1983.

Better Homes and Gardens:
New Baby Book, by Edwin Kiester, Jr., and Sally Valente Kiester. Des Moines: Meredith Corp., 1985.
Stretching Living Space. Des Moines: Meredith Corp., 1983.
Your Family Centers. Des Moines: Meredith Corp., 1983.
Your Walls & Ceilings. Des Moines: Meredith Corp., 1983.

Bollinger, Taree, and Patricia Cramer, *The Baby Gear Guide*. Reading, Mass.: Addison-Wesley Publishing Co., 1985.

Brookes, John, *The Garden Book*. New York: Crown Publishers, 1984.

Chase, Richard A., M.D., John J. Fisher III, and Richard R. Rubin, eds., *Your Baby: The First Wondrous Year*. New York: Collier Books, 1984.

Clarke-Stewart, Alison, and Susan Friedman, *Child Development: Infancy through Adolescence*. New York: John Wiley & Sons, 1984.

Conran, Terence:
The Bed and Bath Book. New York: Crown Publishers, 1978.
The House Book. New York: Crown Publishers, 1983.

Crane, Catherine C., *What Do You Say to a Naked Room?* New York: Dial Press, 1979.

Fisher, John J., *Toys to Grow with*. New York: Perigee Book, 1986.

Foa, Linda, and Geri Brin, *Kids' Stuff*. New York: Pantheon Books, 1979.

Frost, Joe L., and Barry L. Klein, *Children's Play and Playgrounds*. Boston: Allyn and Bacon, 1979.

Galvin, Patrick J., *Successful Space Saving at Home*. Farmington, Mich.: Structures Publishing Co., 1976.

Gelson, Hilary, *Children about the House*. London: Design Council, 1976.

Gilliatt, Mary:
The Decorating Book. New York: Pantheon Books, 1981.
Designing Rooms for Children. Boston: Little, Brown and Co., 1985.

Gilliatt, Mary, Susan Zevon, and Michael W. Robbins, *Decorating on the Cheap*. New York: Workman Publishing, 1984.

Gillis, Jack, and Mary Ellen R. Fise, *The Childwise Catalog: A Consumer Guide to Buying the Safest and Best Products for Your Children*. New York: Pocket Books, 1986.

Glazer, Robin Kriegsman, *Letting Go*. Secaucus, N.J.: Citadel Press, 1983.

Green, Martin I., *A Sigh of Relief: The First-Aid Handbook for Childhood Emergencies*. New York: Bantam Books, 1984.

Hague, William E., ed., *The New Complete Basic Book of Home Decorating*. Garden City, N.Y.: Doubleday & Co., 1982.

Haven, Sharon Owen, *Room to Grow: Making Your Child's Bedroom an Exciting World*. Berkeley, Calif.: Two Step Books, 1979.

Hoppert, Rita, *Rings, Swings & Climbing Things*. Chicago: Contemporary Books, 1985.

The How to Clean Handbook. Cincinnati: Procter & Gamble Educational Services, 1986.

Innes, Jocasta, *Paint Magic*. New York: Pantheon Books, 1987.

Jones, Sandy, *Good Things for Babies*. Boston: Houghton Mifflin Co., 1980.

Kelly, Marguerite, and Elia Parsons, *The Mother's Almanac*. Garden City, N.Y.: Doubleday & Co., 1975.

Levine, Ellen, *Children's Rooms: How to Decorate Them to Grow with Your Child*. Indianapolis: Bobbs-Merrill, 1975.

Liman, Ellen, *Babyspace: A Guide for Growing Families with Shrinking Space*. New York: Perigee Books, 1983.

Liman, Ellen, and Carol Panter, *Decorating Your Room: A Do-It-Yourself Guide*. New York: Franklin Watts, 1974.

McCullough, Bonnie Runyan, and Susan Walker Monson, *401 Ways to Get Your Kids to Work at Home*. New York: St. Martin's Press, 1981.

McGrath, Molly, and Norman McGrath, *Children's Spaces: 50 Architects & Designers Create Environments for the Young*. New York: William Morrow and Co., 1978.

Maguire, Jack:
Kids' Rooms: Imaginative Ideas for Creating the Perfect Space for Your Child. Tucson, Ariz.: HPBooks, 1987.
Outdoor Spaces: Landscape Design for Today's Living. New York: Henry Holt and Co., 1987.

Miller, Peggy L., *Creative Outdoor Play Areas*. Englewood Cliffs, N.J.: Prentice-Hall, 1972.

Mills, Jean, *Babyworks: Every Parent's Sourcebook for Essential Baby Paraphernalia*. New York: Viking, 1985.

Montessori, Maria, *The Absorbent Mind*. Translated from the Italian by Claude A. Claremont. New York: Holt, Rinehart and Winston, 1967.

Mueser, Anne Marie, and George E. Verrilli, M.D., *Welcome Baby: A Guide to the First Six Weeks*. New York: St. Martin's Press, 1982.

Mussen, Paul Henry, et al., *Child Development and Personality*. New York: Harper & Row, 1984.

The New Apartment Book, by the Editors of *Apartment Life* magazine. New York: Harmony Books, 1983.

Ostrow, Albert A., *Planning Your Home for Play*. Atlanta: Tupper & Love, 1954.

Princeton Center for Infancy, *The Parenting Advisor*. Garden City, N.Y.: Anchor Books, 1978.

Reit, Seymour V., *Sibling Rivalry*. New York: Ballantine Books, 1985.

Rosenberg, Stephen N., M.D., *The Johnson & Johnson First Aid Book*. New York: Warner Books, 1985.

Salk, Lee, *The Complete Dr. Salk*. New York: World Almanac Publications, 1984.

Schoen, Elin, *The Closet Book*. New York: Harmony Books, 1982.

Schram, Joseph F., *Successful Children's Rooms*. Farmington, Mich.: Structures Publishing Co., 1979.

Sills, Barbara, and Jeanne Henry, *The Mother to Mother Baby Care Book*. New York: Avon Books, 1981.

Smith, Peter K., ed., *Children's Play: Research Developments and Practical Applications*. New York: Gordon and Breach Science Publishers, 1986.

Stoddard, Alexandra, *A Child's Place: How to Create a Living Environment for Your Child*. Garden City, N.Y.: Doubleday & Co., 1977.

Stoppard, Miriam, *Day by Day Baby Care*. New York: Villard Books, 1983.

Storage, by the Editors of Time-Life Books (Your Home series). Alexandria, Va.: Time-Life Books, 1985.

Sullivan, S. Adams, *The Father's Almanac*. Garden City, N.Y.: Doubleday & Co., 1980.

Sunset Books:
Children's Rooms & Play Yards. Menlo Park, Calif.: Lane Publishing Co., 1980.
Garage, Attic & Basement Storage. Menlo Park, Calif.: Lane Publishing Co., 1982.
Ideas for Bedroom & Bath Storage. Menlo Park, Calif.: Lane Publishing Co., 1982.
Ideas for Storage. Menlo Park, Calif.: Lane Publishing Co., 1975.

Making Your Home Child-Safe, by Don Vandervort. Menlo Park, Calif.: Lane Publishing Co., 1988.

Woodworking Projects II. Menlo Park, Calif.: Lane Publishing Co., 1984.

Touw, Kathleen, *Parent Tricks-of-the-Trade.* Washington, D.C.: Acropolis Books, 1981.

Winston, Stephanie, *Getting Organized: The Easy Way to Put Your Life in Order.* New York: W. W. Norton & Co., 1978.

Zigler, Edward F., and Matia Finn-Stevenson, *Children: Development and Social Issues.* Lexington, Mass.: D. C. Heath and Co., 1987.

PERIODICALS

Berman, Claire, "Learning to Live with a Sloppy Kid." *Parents,* November 1987.

Bethany, Marilyn, "What Do Children Want?" *The New York Times Magazine,* March 15, 1981.

Brin, Geri, "Conquering Space." *Parents,* April 1983.

Caldwell, Jean, "Safety Begins at Home." *American Baby,* January 1985.

Coen, Patricia, and Bryan Milford, "Make Room!" *Redbook,* March 1988.

Colby, Suzanne, "The Enemy within the Home." *Baby Talk,* October 1985.

Cook, Gregory D., "Fun for Kids! Two Great Projects You Can Build." *Better Homes and Gardens,* February 1988.

Copple, Carol, "The Two-Home Child." *Sesame Street Magazine,* January/February 1988.

Farrant, Alan W., "3 for the Outdoors: Children's Play Box." *Popular Mechanics,* May 1982.

Fulton, Alice, and Pauline Hatch, "Creating a Kid-Ready Room." *Mothering,* Fall 1985.

George, F. Holland, "Festive Family Traditions." *American Baby,* December 1987.

Gillis, Jack, and Mary Ellen R. Fise, "The ABC's of Safe Parenting." *Good Housekeeping,* September 1987.

"Health Briefs: Children + Lighters = Danger." *Baby Talk,* February 1988.

Holcomb, Betty, "Child Safety Is Up to You." *Parents,* March 1988.

"Home Safety Guidelines: In the First Aid Kit." *Baby Talk,* May 1988.

Isaacs, Susan, "Helping Your Kids Get Organized." *Parents,* May 1983.

Kass, Benny L., "Get Written Home-Improvement Contracts." *The Washington Post,* January 30, 1988.

Kelly, Kate, "Preventing Electrical Accidents." *Parents,* December 1985.

Leardi, Jeanette, "Playing It Safe." *Sesame Street Magazine,* June 1988.

Lovell, Penny, and Thelma Harms, "How Can Playgrounds Be Improved?" *Young Children,* March 1985.

"March Almanac: Caring for Silk." *American Baby,* February 1988.

Menke, Stephen, "Build PM's Super Sandbox." *Popular Mechanics,* April 1980.

Miller, Stuart, "Designing the Home for Children: A Need-Based Approach." *Children's Environments Quarterly,* Spring 1986.

Muenchow, Susan, "Kids & Safety." *Parents,* April 1984.

Nolan, William L., "Super Solutions for Kids' Room Clutter." *Better Homes and Gardens,* January 1985.

Provey, Joseph R., and Conrad Stowers, "In-Ground Sandbox You Can Build in One Session." *Popular Mechanics,* August 1981.

Pushkar, Robert G., "What Baby Sees." *Parents,* March 1988.

"Quest for Cash: Tracking the Elusive Remodeling Buck." *Remodeling Ideas,* Spring 1988.

"Remodeling: What It Costs, How to Pay for It." *Changing Times,* March 1986.

Shelov, Steven P., M.D., "Pediatric Update." *Child,* November/December 1987.

Smith, Clinton, "Designers' Sketchbook: Beyond the Sandbox." *Home,* June 1987.

Smith, Dian G., "Room for One More." *Sesame Street Magazine,* January/February 1988.

Sousa, Jan Hart, "A Child-Proof Home." *Parents,* February 1985.

Toufexis, Anastasia, "Johnny Appleseed of the Swing Set." *Time,* December 15, 1986.

Trunzo, Candace E., "A Savvy Borrower's Shopping Guide." *Money,* April 1987.

OTHER PUBLICATIONS

Baker, Katherine Read, "Let's Play Outdoors." Washington, D.C.: National Association for the Education of Young Children, 1966.

Caldwell, Jean, "How to Childproof Your Home." Knoxville, Tenn.: Parenting Adviser Information Center, 1985.

"Consumer Information for CCA Pressure-Treated Wood." Troy, Va.: Valley Timber Sales, no date.

A Handbook of Child Safety: Emergency Phone Numbers. Gerber Products Co., 1981.

Kritchevsky, Sybil, Elizabeth Prescott, and Lee Walling, "Planning Environments for Young Children." Washington, D.C.: National Association for the Education of Young Children, 1986.

"Safety Requirements for Home Playground Equipment." Voluntary Product Standard PS 66-75. Washington, D.C.: National Bureau of Standards, U.S. Department of Commerce, July 1976.

U.S. Consumer Product Safety Commission:

Consumer Product Safety Alert: Danger—Children and Lighters. Washington, D.C., June 1987.

General Guidelines for New and Existing Playgrounds. Vol. 1 of *A Handbook for Public Playground Safety.* Washington, D.C., no date.

Home Electrical Safety Audit. Washington, D.C., October 1984.

On the Side of Safety: Caution! Choosing and Using Your Gas Space Heater. Washington, D.C., September 1985.

Product Safety Fact Sheet No. 9: Ranges and Ovens. Washington, D.C., March 1987.

Product Safety Fact Sheet No. 16: Extension Cords and Wall Outlets. Washington, D.C., December 1982.

Product Safety Fact Sheet No. 18: The Home Electrical System. Washington, D.C., November 1983.

Product Safety Fact Sheet No. 34: Space Heaters. Washington, D.C., September 1985.

Product Safety Fact Sheet No. 54: Electric Baseboard Heaters. Washington, D.C., February 1980.

Product Safety Fact Sheet No. 61: Electrically Operated Toys and Children's Articles. Washington, D.C., September 1979.

Product Safety Fact Sheet No. 71: Bunk Beds. Washington, D.C., October 1987.

Product Safety Fact Sheet No. 98: Electric Space Heaters. Washington, D.C., November 1984.

Product Safety Fact Sheet No. 99: Ground Fault Circuit Interrupters. Washington, D.C., December 1985.

Product Safety Update: Using a Portable Heater? Use a Smoke Detector, Too. Washington, D.C., October 7, 1987.

The Safe Nursery. Washington, D.C., August 1986.

What You Should Know about Home Fire Safety. Washington, D.C., October 1983.

What You Should Know about Smoke Detectors. Washington, D.C., April 1982.

Your Home Fire Safety Checklist. Washington, D.C., September 1987.

Acknowledgments and Picture Credits

The editors are particularly indebted to the following people: Jill Kaplan, New York, N.Y., who served as consultant on Color's Transforming Magic, page 26; Norman Oehlke, International Fabricare Institute, Silver Spring, Md., who served as consultant on the stain chart, page 37.

The editors are also indebted to the following people for their creative contributions to this volume: Alice Cannon, Alexandria, Va.; Sandy Huke, Rockville, Md.; Lea Jeffers, Alexandria, Va.; Beecie Kupersmith, Alexandria, Va.; Augusta Moravec Interiors, Washington, D.C.; Mary Rust, Alexandria, Va.

The editors also thank: John Preston, U.S. Consumer Product Safety Commission, Washington, D.C.

The sources for the photographs in this book are listed below, followed by the sources for the illustrations. Credits from left to right are separated by semicolons, from top to bottom by dashes.

Photographs. Cover, 4-7: Roger Foley. 15: Beecie Kupersmith. 39: Roger Foley. 63: Beecie Kupersmith. 69: Roger Foley. 99: Roger Foley. 119: Roger Foley. 121: Beecie Kupersmith.

Illustrations. 8-19: Art by Donald Gates from photos by Beecie Kupersmith. 20: Art by Donald Gates from photo by Marilyn Segall. 21: Art by Beecie Kupersmith—art by Donald Gates from photo by Beecie Kupersmith. 26, 27: Art by William Hennessy from photos by Beecie Kupersmith. 29-31: Art by Donald Gates from photos by Beecie Kupersmith. 32: Art by William Hennessy from photos by Beecie Kupersmith. 34: Art by Donald Gates from photo by Beecie Kupersmith. 41: Art by Elizabeth Wolf from photo by Jane Jordan. 42-52: Art by Elizabeth Wolf from photos by Beecie Kupersmith. 53: Art by Fred Holz. 54-57: Art by Elizabeth Wolf from photos by Beecie Kupersmith. Wrapping paper, page 57, by Gordon Frazer. 58: Art by Elizabeth Wolf from photo by Marilyn Segall. 60, 61: Art by Elizabeth Wolf from photo by Jane Jordan. 62: Art by Elizabeth Wolf from photo by Beecie Kupersmith. 64, 65: Art by Fred Holz from photo by Beecie Kupersmith; art by William Hennessy from photo by Beecie Kupersmith. 67: Art by Fred Holz from photo by Beecie Kupersmith. 70-75: Art by Lisa F. Semerad from photos by Beecie Kupersmith. 77: Art by William Hennessy from photo by Ellyn Sudow. 78: Art by William Hennessy from photos by Beecie Kupersmith (2)—art by William Hennessy from photo by Jane Jordan. 79-81: Art by William Hennessy from photos by Beecie Kupersmith. 83: Art by Lisa F. Semerad from photo by Marilyn Segall. 84, 86: Art by Lisa F. Semerad from photos by Beecie Kupersmith. 87: Art by Lisa F. Semerad from photo by Jane Jordan. 88-91: Art by Lisa F. Semerad from photos by Beecie Kupersmith. 93: Art by William Hennessy from photo by Lee/Rowan ®. 94: Art by William Hennessy from photos by Jane Jordan. 95-97: Art by William Hennessy from photos by Beecie Kupersmith. 101: Art by Marguerite E. Bell from photo by Ellyn Sudow. 102, 103: Art by Marguerite E. Bell from photo by Beecie Kupersmith. 104: Art by Marguerite E. Bell from photo by Linda Rose. Architect Jennifer Bender-Moran. 105: Art by Marguerite E. Bell from photo by Jane Jordan. 106, 107: Art by Marguerite E. Bell from photos by Ellyn Sudow. 108, 109: Art by Marguerite E. Bell from photos by Jane Jordan. 110-115: Art by Marguerite E. Bell from photos by Ellyn Sudow. 116, 117: Art by Marguerite E. Bell from photo by Marilyn Segall. 122, 123: Art by Lisa F. Semerad from photos by Marilyn Segall. 124, 125: Art by Lisa F. Semerad from photos by Beecie Kupersmith. 126-130: Art by Lisa F. Semerad from photos by Marilyn Segall. 132: Art by Lisa F. Semerad from photo by Beecie Kupersmith. 135: Art by Lisa F. Semerad from photo by Linda Rose. 136: Art by Lisa F. Semerad from photo by Marilyn Segall.

Props: Cover: baskets, American Artisan, Inc., Alexandria, Va.; pillowcases, Palais Royal, Alexandria, Va.; quilt, Rocky Road to Kansas, Alexandria, Va. 7: rug, Conran's, Washington, D.C. 78: wagon, America!, Alexandria, Va.

Index